FLORIDA'S FABULOUS FLICKS

Hollywood EAST

FLORIDA'S FABULOUS FLICKS

JAMES PONTI

TRIBUNE PUBLISHING
1992

Edited by Kathleen M. Kiely and Dixie Kasper
Designed by Bill Henderson
Production by Ken Paskman
Author's photo by Frank Busby
Photographed at General Cinema, Colonial Promenade,
Orlando, Florida

Movie photos provided by
Film Favorites
PO Box 133
Canton, OK 73724
and The Orlando Sentinel.
The photos in this book were provided to the public for promotional purposes at the time of
the movies' release, by the film companies listed in this book. We regret any inadvertent
omissions, and will correct them in a future edition.

Printed in the United States

First Edition: May 1992

Library of Congress
Catalog Card Number:
92-060806

ABOUT THE AUTHOR

James Ponti saw his first movie, *Dr. Terror's House of Horrors*, when he was two days old. He's been going to the movies regularly ever since. A graduate of the University of Southern California film school, Mr. Ponti grew up in Atlantic Beach, Florida. He co-wrote screenplays for the films *King's Ransom* and *Even Angels Fall,* and has written for the Nickelodeon cable network, for the television show *The Adventures of Superboy* and for various publications. He comments on the film industry each week for public radio. Mr. Ponti lives in Orlando with his wife and their dog.

To Denise

CONTENTS

INTRODUCTION

The movies and I are both European imports that took root in Florida: Filmmaking was born in France, and I was born in Italy. When I was a baby, my family moved to Jacksonville, Florida, where the film industry developed during its pre-Hollywood infancy. Like the movies, I left Jacksonville for the lure of Los Angeles and, like the movies, I came back to Florida to beat California's high cost of living.

My relationship with the movies began on March 26, 1966, when my mother took me to see *Dr. Terror's House of Horrors* at a movie house in Pisa, Italy. I was only two days old, but something must have clicked, because I've been going to the movies non-stop ever since. I practically grew up inside the Royal Palm Theater in Atlantic Beach, Florida. Movies were the perfect antidote to the Florida summer—the theater was air-conditioned and my house wasn't.

I left Florida to study screenwriting at the University of Southern California. As a freshman, I was asked by a fellow student what it was like to live in a state where everyone is older than sixty. I didn't realize it then, but this was the first of a four-year string of questions about Florida that would have nothing in common but their media-induced absurdity.

In the ensuing years, I had to explain that I had never been in a drug-related shootout in Miami, I didn't drive around in an air boat and, although he was a cool guy, Burt Reynolds wasn't the governor.

People's perceptions of the Sunshine State had been distorted, in part, by years of film and television viewing. This is one side effect of Florida's long involvement with the film industry.

Once leery of Hollywood, Florida today is actively trying to expand its role in the movies. But many people are unaware that the state already has a rich history on the silver screen. This book provides an unusual look at the state's hundred-year romance with motion pictures.

I am indebted to a number of people who helped me write this book. Thanks to fellow writers Bill Kelley, Richard Alan Nelson and Bob Morris, as well as to Dixie, Kathy and everyone else at Tribune Publishing for keeping me on the right track.

I owe a great deal of thanks (and overdue book fines) to Max Brown, and to everyone at the Arts and Literature reference desk at the Orlando Public Library and at the Florida Room of the Miami Public Library. Thanks also to Mark Mullen and Sigi Tiedtke.

The local film offices provided invaluable assistance. I am especially grateful to Elizabeth Wentworth in Fort Lauderdale, Deeny Kaplan in Miami, Chuck Elderd in Palm Beach and Virginia Pantico in Key West.

Finally, I am indebted to Denise, Sylvia, Carey, Terence, Laurie and Cathy for all of their input, help and support.

I hope you will enjoy what you read.

James Ponti

Hollywood EAST

PREVIEW

WITNESS THE SPECTACLE THAT IS FLORIDA!

I t's FLORIDA! Now in TROPIC THRILLVISION. With a cast of thousands and more stars than there are in the heavens. Featuring John Wayne and Donna Reed as the war-torn lovers! William Hurt and Kathleen Turner as the lawyer and his evil mistress! Elvis Presley and Tom Cruise as the death-defying racers! With special appearances by Spencer Tracy as Lieutenant Colonel Jimmy Doolittle and Jimmy Stewart as Buttons the Clown.

FLORIDA! Coming soon to a theater near you ...

Florida and the movies—It's a love affair as old as filmmaking itself. The story began almost a century ago, in 1898, with the Spanish-American War news-reels *U.S. Cavalry Supplies Unloading at Tampa Florida* and *Transport Ships at Port Tampa*. Since then, the state has seen Jacksonville emerge, then fade away, as an early film center, and Orlando strive to become the Tinseltown of the East.

A festival of Florida films would include classics like *30 Seconds Over Tokyo*, recent hits like *Parenthood*, B pictures like *Creature from the Black Lagoon* and all-time duds like *Honky Tonk Freeway*. Late-night viewing might even include a screening of the porno classic *Deep Throat*.

Production companies have gone on location just about everywhere in the state, from Pensacola, on the end of the Panhandle, to the southernmost tip of Key West. Big cities, small neighborhoods, gover-nors, aspiring starlets — all have done whatever they could to become part of the magic, glamour and excitement that make up the movies.

That excitment took hold in Jacksonville at the turn of the century. The city was Hollywood's chief rival in attracting film production companies escaping the cold winters of New York and the strong arm of The Motion Pictures Patents Company, which controlled the industry.

Kalem, Gaumont, Klutho, Edison and Biograph were the Universals and MGMs of their day. They were among more than thirty silent film companies based in Jacksonville when it was known as "The Winter Film Capital of the World." During this period, the city saw the likes of The Keystone Kops, Oliver Hardy and Lionel Barrymore begin their careers.

As the industry grew, however, the companies often found themselves out of step with Jacksonville's conservative ways. Local residents and religious leaders were getting fed up with the way the movie people ran roughshod over the town. For example, one production crew needed a shot of a fire engine racing down the street, so they just called in a phony alarm and waited for the hook and ladder to come to their rescue. Church groups became upset that bank robberies were filmed on Sundays.

Safety also became a major concern. After the filming of a riot scene for the film *The Clarion,* a real riot broke out. Forty policemen were called onto the scene to calm more than 1,300 extras. Stunt filming for the movie *The Dead Alive* raised eyebrows when a car sped down Main Street and plunged into the St. Johns River. Exhibiting the callousness of the industry, the director filmed the scene last in case the actors didn't survive the crash.

Such behavior made the film industry the primary

debate in Jacksonville's mayoral election of 1917. The conservatives were pitted against film booster and incumbent Mayor "Jet" Bowden. When Bowden lost the election, the film companies took it as an ominous sign of their standing in Jacksonville. Meanwhile, California offered friendlier arrangements, better weather and a more diverse terrain. Within a few years, all the companies had fled west.

In Los Angeles, the film industry took root. The most successful production companies built large studios to handle all of their filming needs. One exception was United Artists, which was

formed by Charlie Chaplin, Mary Pickford, Douglas Fairbanks and D.W. Griffith. With no studio to call home, UA filmed on location. In 1929, they ventured all the way to Tampa to shoot the film *Hell Harbor*. This early talkie, which starred Jean Hersholt, launched the state's renaissance as a location.

Although it wasn't home to the film companies, Florida could offer locations unavailable in California. This was true in 1941, when MGM sent Spencer Tracy, Anne Revere and Claude Eckman to Florida to make *The Yearling*. It seemed only natural that the filming take place in the same wilderness that inspired Marjorie Kinnan Rawlings to write her novel. But the wilderness is not a good place for filmmaking, and the production was a disaster.

The cast and crew were inundated with bugs, and young Eckman and the fawn were growing too fast. Moreover, Tracy was miserable because he couldn't find a good bar, and he and director Victor Fleming had knock-down fights. Florida's reputation in Hollywood was dissolving, and might have been ruined had it not been for the outbreak of World War II. The war mercifully halted filming of *The*

Yearling, but it also dramatically increased production in the state.

Like the Cavalry had done in 1898, the military brought cameras back to Florida in the early '40s. GIs shipped out to theaters of war abroad, and Hollywood brought the war home to theaters across America. The government asked the studios to help boost the nation's morale, and opened military bases to movie stars and camera crews to support the cause. But bases in California were considered a possible target of Japanese attack, so the filmmakers had to go elsewhere.

Florida was a natural solution — it had numerous military installations, and a subtropical terrain that could double for the Pacific islands being portrayed in the movies. *Air Force, A Guy Named Joe, They Were Expendable, 30 Seconds Over Tokyo* and *Twelve O'Clock High* are among the war classics that were shot in Florida. They were all supremely successful, as entertainment and as propaganda.

That success helped lift the stain left on Florida when *The Yearling* canceled production. At war's end, America wanted pure entertainment, and the studios began to venture beyond California more often. Florida's lush tropical settings offered a perfect backdrop for escapist fare like the Esther Williams aqua-ballets. MGM even returned to make *The Yearling*, this time with Gregory Peck, Jane Wyman and Claude Jarman, Jr.

Competition also drove the studios looking for more action. Worried that they might lose their audience to television, moviemakers offered exotic locations and technological advances that the small screen could never rival. One such technique was the wide-screen format called CinemaScope, which made the TV screen seem even smaller. Among the first CinemaScope pictures was *Beneath the 12 Mile Reef*, filmed in Key West and Tarpon Springs.

Another experiment in technology was the short-lived 3-D effect. Wearing special glasses, audiences could watch films that were seemingly three-dimensional. Unfortunately, the process was cumbersome, and it was only succesful as a novelty for science fiction and monster films like *Creature from the Black Lagoon*. Filmed at Wakulla Springs in 1954, *Creature* saved Universal from impending bankruptcy. The studio's success paid off for Florida three decades later, when Universal built a giant theme park/studio in Orlando.

In the mid-'50s, Hollywood stopped fighting progress, and decided to embrace television. Rather than diminish the movie audience, the small screen created an even greater demand for production. In Florida, this was best felt in Miami, which became a center for both film and television production.

Miami's international recognition and holiday atmosphere were perfectly suited to the movies and TV. Stars like Frank Sinatra and Jerry Lewis had long retreated to South Florida for vacations — making movies there was a natural progression. Jackie Gleason liked Miami so much he had his television studios relocated there. Meanwhile, the Ivan Tors Studio in North Miami was producing movies and television shows like *Flipper* and *Gentle Ben*.

Despite Miami's success, and continued

filming throughout the state, Florida failed to take full advantage of the opportunities presented by the film industry. This attitude was disastrous in 1974, when native son Burt Reynolds tried to make *The Longest Yard* in the Sunshine State.

Even though he was the world's top movie star at the time, Reynolds was unable to cut through the red tape in his home state, and had to move the production to neighboring Georgia. (Ever the local booster, he still kept Florida as the setting of the movie.) Such PR debacles led to the creation of the Florida Film Bureau and regional film offices.

Unwilling to lose out completely like it did in 1917, Florida has agressively fought to increase its share of the film industry. Skyrocketing production budgets have sent the studios looking for alternatives to California and New York. They most often come looking in Florida, North Carolina, Texas and Illinois, where they are greeted by user-friendly governments and cheap labor.

When Reynolds returned to scout locations for *Smokey and the Bandit II*, Florida was ready. Looking for a bridge to blow up, he was offered two bridges by Orlando officials, who enthusiastically suggested that the script be rewritten to destroy both.

This generous cooperation has continued through the years. In the town of Mount Dora, entire buildings were painted pink for the 1981 film *Honky Tonk Freeway*. Likewise, a whole neighborhood in the Carpenter's Run subdivision north of Tampa got a Crayola paint job and had giant topiary creations placed in their front yards for *Edward Scissorhands*.

After *Miami Vice* became the most popular show on television, Florida production grew by leaps and bounds. The show reinvented South Florida in the minds of America, suggesting fresh, new possibilities for filming.

The trend was sealed a few years later, when two Hollywood stalwarts established full-service production facilities in Orlando. The Disney/MGM Studios opened in 1989, and Universal Studios followed suit a year later.

The opening of the studios marked a new era for Florida and for motion pictures, as the state moves beyond ocassional location roles. In the past few years, Florida has fostered productions ranging from big-budget feature films like *Cape Fear* to the children's cable network Nickelodeon.

Steadily, Florida has emerged as the leader among the Hollywood alternatives, ranking behind only California and New York in film and television production. The state's non-union business climate keeps costs down, while experienced crews and state-of-the-art facilities maintain quality.

Some industry insiders, called "bi-coastal" when they commuted between New York and California, have become "tri-coastal" as they've added Florida to their loop. In fact, Florida has become so confident in its role in the film industry that a new nickname has emerged: HOLLYWOOD EAST.

ROLL CAMERA

WHAT'S A FLORIDA FILM?

It seems a simple question with an obvious answer. A Florida film is a movie made in Florida. Ask any number of people to name a Florida film, and odds are that the two most common responses will be *Key Largo* and *Tarzan*. Good answers, but not quite correct.

Sure, Key Largo is a place in Florida, and there was a movie about it. You can rest assured that a number of restaurants and hotels on the island have pictures of Humphrey Bogart and Lauren Bacall on their walls. But *Key Largo* was made in California, and this is a book about movies made in Florida.

The same goes for *Tarzan*. Growing up in Florida, I would have bet my life that Johnny Weissmuller was the honorary mayor of Silver Springs. As it turns out, most of the Tarzan movies were also shot in California. A few of the films shot scenes in Florida, but for the most part the legend has far outgrown the truth.

On the flip side, some movies you'd never think of are bona fide Florida films. *They Were Expendable*, the John Wayne movie about Navy patrol boats in the Philippines, seems to have nothing to do with the Sunshine State. But since a war was raging in the real Philippines, most of the film was shot in then-look-alike Key Biscayne. *30 Seconds Over Tokyo*, shot at Eglin Air Force Base, was another Florida-based World War II movie. The remake of *Cape Fear* was filmed around Fort Lauderdale, and *Body Heat* was done in Palm Beach and Hollywood, Florida.

The following is a list of sound-era feature films, made for theatrical release, that were shot at least partially in Florida. The listings include the film's studio, year of release, principal locations, behind-the-camera talent and cast members. It is not meant to be an encyclopedic listing of every movie that ever shot a single frame in Florida. Rather, it offers a detailed and enjoyable look at the Sunshine State's diverse participation in the movies.

ABSENCE OF MALICE (Columbia - 1981)

Miami
Written by Kurt Luedtke
Directed by Sydney Pollack
Starring Paul Newman, Sally Field, Melinda Dillon, Wilford Brimley

"Suppose you picked up this morning's newspaper and your life was a front page headline... And everything they said was accurate... But none of it was true."

"The D.A., Feds and the police set her up to write the story that explodes his world. Now he's going to write the book on getting even."

With a poster synopsis this long, it's amazing they found room for pictures.

Critics have rapped *Absence of Malice*, claiming that the film presents an unrealistic portrayal of a big-city newspaper, seemingly devoid of integrity and control over its reporters. Of course, many critics work at big-city newspapers and might be a little sensitive about the subject.

In the film, Sally Field is a journalist who writes a series of articles that implicates Paul Newman, the son of a mobster, in the disappearance of a union leader. The only problem is that he's innocent. The central issue of the story is the responsibility of the press with regard to the rights of the accused.

Paul Newman

Journalists felt especially betrayed by screenwriter Kurt Luedtke, who once served as executive editor of the *Detroit Free Press*. But, while the *Miami Standard* may not seem realistic, it's important to note that Hollywood and realism have little in common. Faster than you can say "job envy," Luedtke and his script were nominated for an Academy Award. (He would win an Oscar four years later for his script for *Out of Africa*.)

Originally set in Detroit, the plot was refitted to Florida so that production could avoid the harsh Michigan winter. Director Sydney Pollack chose Miami over Tampa after scouting both locations. Much of the filming was done at the *Miami Herald*, where Luedtke was once a general assignments reporter.

(See "On Location")

AIR FORCE (Warner Brothers - 1943)

Tampa
Written by Dudley Nichols
Directed by Howard Hawks
Starring John Ridgely, Gig Young, Arthur Kennedy, Harry Carey, John Garfield

"They're pretty good when they've got the edge, ten or twelve to one. They don't like an even fight, though."
Line from American pilot trying to make other flyers (and the audience) feel better about the war.

"I would hate to think that it couldn't happen—or didn't— because it certainly leaves you feeling awful good."
New York Times reviewer Bosley Crowther showing that the line worked.

Considered by many to be the first great World War II movie, *Air Force* follows the crew of the *Mary Ann*, a B-17 Flying Fortress that arrives in Hawaii just as the Japanese are attacking Pearl

Harbor. The crew goes on to fight in various bat-
tles, all the while providing opportunities to
showcase heroic views of the American GI in the
Pacific.

Made at the request of the U.S. Army Air Corps
(which would not become the Air Force until 1947),
the film was directed by Howard Hawks, who had
been a pilot with the Air Corps in World War I.
Stagecoach screenwriter Dudley Nichols wrote the
screenplay and novelist William Faulkner helped on
a few scenes.

Rather than shoot at a California base close to the
war in the Pacific, the cast and crew spent eight
weeks filming at Drew Air Field, outside Tampa. The
biggest production difficulty was securing military
hardware while the nation was at war. For exteriors
of the *Mary Ann*, the filmmakers had the use of an
actual B-17, which was later lost in the Pacific.
Interiors were shot on a $40,000 model that was
specially constructed not to give away the secrets
and weaknesses of the aircraft.

(See "On Location")

AIRPORT '77 (Universal - 1977)

Miami
Written by Michael Scheff, David Spector
Directed by Jerry Jameson
Starring James Stewart

The third of four *Airport* films, *Airport '77* plays
like a greatest hits album of disaster movies. It
begins with the hijacking of an airplane
(*Airport*), which then crashes beneath the surface of
the water (*The Poseidon Adventure*), trapping a group
representing every potential audience demographic
(*Towering Inferno*) on a continental shelf that is slowly giving way (*Earthquake*).

As in all disaster movies, there is plenty of intertwining melodrama, an all-star cast and the requisite appearance by George Kennedy. On land, James Stewart plays the plane's owner; his home is Miami's Vizcaya mansion.

ALL FALL DOWN (MGM - 1962)

Key West
Written by William Inge
Directed by John Frankenheimer
Starring Warren Beatty, Brandon de Wilde

In the critically acclaimed *All Fall Down*, Warren Beatty is a a dissolute young man, while Brandon de Wilde portrays the younger brother who worships him. His hero worship is cut short when he sees the effect of Beatty's callousness on visitor Eva Marie Saint, who falls for him. In early scenes, Key West doubles for the fictional Key Bonita.

Angela Lansbury, Karl Malden, Eva Marie Saint, Warren Beatty and Brandon de Wilde

Although Beatty played the lead role of Berry-Berry, at the time he was probably the least known member of the cast, which also featured Karl Malden and Angela Lansbury. During production, newspaper articles still identified him by his most noteworthy trait—as Shirley MacLaine's brother.

That same year, however, *Splendor in the Grass* made him an instant movie star at twenty-four. This was already his third pairing with the Pulitzer Prize-winning author William Inge. He starred in both of the playwright's screenplays, *Splendor in the Grass* and *All Fall Down*, and in his Broadway production of *A Loss of Roses*.

ANGEL BABY (Allied Artists - 1960)

Homestead
Written by Oris Borstem, Samuel Roeca, Paul Mason
Directed by Paul Wendkos
Starring Joan Blondell, George Hamilton, Mercedes McCambridge, Burt Reynolds, Salome Jens

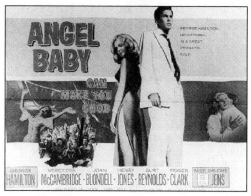

Poster for *Angel Baby*

Like *All Fall Down*, *Angel Baby* is a melodrama that features an unknown cast member who would later rise to superstardom. This time it's Burt Reynolds, making his film debut as the unscrupulous Hoke Adams, who exploits a mute girl cured by evangelist George Hamilton.

Although their personas couldn't be more different, Reynolds and Hamilton are both from the Palm Beach area. Hamilton had already made a splash in *Where the Boys Are* in nearby Fort Lauderdale. While the film was being made, *Angel Baby*'s producers claimed that it was the first feature film shot entirely in the Miami area.

AROUND THE WORLD UNDER THE SEA (MGM - 1966)

Miami
Written by Art Arthur, Arthur Weiss
Directed by Andrew Marton, Ricou Browning
Starring Lloyd Bridges, Shirley Eaton, Keenan Wynn, Gary Merrill

Around the World Under the Sea is one of numerous projects produced in Florida by Ivan Tors, who set up a North Miami studio that specialized in family entertainment. Like many of Tors' film and television projects (*Flipper, Hello Down There*), this film is built around an aquatic theme. In the film, Lloyd Bridges leads an expedition along the ocean floor to research underwater volcanoes.

The excellent underwater sequences were directed by Ricou Browning. Browning had been a Tallahassee lifeguard before being cast to play the creature in the underwater scenes of *Creature from the Black Lagoon*. After *Creature*, he left lifeguarding to pursue a career in filmmaking. It turned out to be a wise decision. His diverse resume includes writing the original *Flipper* story and eventually becoming president of the Ivan Tors Studio—making him the only studio executive who ever got paid to say "No horseplay around the pool."

BAHAMA PASSAGE (Paramount - 1941)

Miami
Written by Virginia Van Upp
Directed by Edward Griffith
Starring Madeleine Carroll, Sterling Hayden, Leo G. Carroll

*B**ahama Passage* came to Florida in order to create an exotic and passionate atmosphere. Set in the West Indies, it's a romance about islander Sterling Hayden, who falls in love with Madeleine Carroll, the sophisticated daughter of the local salt mine manager. Carroll and Hayden were cast opposite each other because of fan response to their scenes together in his film debut *Virginia*.

Certain it had a new star, Paramount began billing him as "The Most Beautiful Man in the Movies."

Hayden, however, had different plans. Following *Bahama Passage*, he abruptly left filmmaking to join the Marines and didn't return to the studio until 1947. During his hiatus, Hayden managed to find the time to fight in World War II and marry and divorce co-star Carroll.

BAND OF THE HAND (Columbia - 1986)

Miami
Written by Leo Garen, Jack Baran
Directed by Paul Michael Glaser
Starring Stephen Lang, Michael Carmine

Band of the Hand follows a group of Miami juvenile delinquents who are trained to fight a drug lord. Could the fact that it's a slick, music-filled, pastel-packed action film have anything to do with the success of *Miami Vice*, which at the time happened to be one of the highest-rated shows on television? Maybe it's a coincidence. *Band* was directed by Paul Michael Glaser, the first half of *Starsky and Hutch,* which was a lot like *Miami Vice* without the imported car and fancy clothes.

THE BAREFOOT MAILMAN (Columbia - 1951)

St. Augustine, Naples, Silver Springs, Key Biscayne
Written by James Gunn, Francis Swann
Directed by Earl McEvoy
Starring Robert Cummings, Jerome Courtland, Terry Moore

Poster for
The Barefoot Mailman

The Barefoot Mailman is the screen adaptation of Theodore Pratt's novel about 19th-century Florida. In the title role, Jerome Courtland must carry the mail twenty-two miles on foot from Fort Lauderdale to pioneer Miami. Along the way he meets up with con artist Robert Cummings and the beautiful Terry Moore. They get involved in a battle between beachcombers and settlers.

Two cast members, Will Geer and Ellen Corby, later teamed up to star in the television series *The Waltons*.

BEAUTY AND THE BEAST (Disney - 1991)

Orlando
Written by Linda Woolverton
Directed by Gary Trousdale, Kirk Wise
Voices by Robby Benson, Paige O'Hara, Angela Lansbury, David Ogden Stiers

Just when everyone thought that animation was dead, Disney's *The Little Mermaid* got rave reviews and huge box office, reviving the medium. Then *Beauty and the Beast* went one better by becoming the first animated feature to receive an Oscar nomination for Best Picture. And the best part is that there are no actors to ask for profit sharing. A little over ten minutes of the film were made at the Disney/MGM Studios in Orlando.

Belle and the Beast

Directors Gary Trousdale and Kirk Wise were hired after making the film *Cranium Command*, which is an attraction at Epcot Center. Disney honcho Jeffrey Katzenberg is rumored to have helped rewrite the final scene so that it would elicit even more tears. The stars of the film are the 525 people who worked on the animation, and the songwriting team of Alan Menken and Howard Ashman. Amazingly, three songs from the film were nominated for Academy Awards, and the title song won. The film is dedicated to Ashman, who died of AIDS just before the film was completed.

THE BELLBOY (Paramount - 1960)

Miami Beach
Written and Directed by Jerry Lewis
Starring Jerry Lewis, Milton Berle

Perhaps more than any other film, *The Bellboy* exemplifies the magnitude of Jerry Lewis's stardom at the height of his career. *Cinderfella* was to be released in the summer of 1960, but Paramount decided it was better suited for the Christmas season and postponed the release. Lewis, however, was determined to have a new picture open on the Fourth of July.

Jerry Lewis

In February, he called the studio and told them to send equipment to Miami, where he would be the following week to begin work on a new movie. When asked which project he was working on, he replied "What's the difference?" The studio capitulated, and soon eight trucks loaded with equipment were headed for Florida.

Like a one-man band, Lewis wrote, produced, directed and starred in this story of a hapless bellboy at the famed Fountainebleu Hotel. He completed production in only twenty-nine days, wrapping the day before an actor's strike began, for a total cost of $2,000,000. *The Bellboy* opened on the Fourth of July, and although its running time is a short 72 minutes, the film was one of the top grossing pictures of the year.

The film also helps explain Lewis's much-noted popularity in France and other foreign markets. *The Bellboy* relies almost exclusively on visual humor. In fact, Lewis's character speaks no lines. While this may grow tiresome for American audiences, it eliminates the language barrier for foreign audiences.

The visual nature of Lewis's humor also led to some technological pioneering. *The Bellboy* was one of the first films to employ a tool that has become a fixture of present day film production—a video monitor. Next to his film camera, Lewis placed a television camera, which fed to a closed-circuit television just out of frame. This allowed Lewis to direct himself better while he was performing.

(See "On Location")

BENEATH THE 12 MILE REEF (Fox-1953)

Key West, Tarpon Springs
Written by A.I. Bezzerides
Directed by Robert Webb
Starring Robert Wagner, Terry Moore, Peter Graves

Robert Wagner and
Terry Moore

If Shakespeare had ever visited the Gulf of Mexico, *Romeo and Juliet* might have turned out like *Beneath the 12 Mile Reef*. In this movie, the Montagues are the Greek sponge divers of Tarpon Springs, and the Capulets are the "Conch" (as Key West natives are known) sponge divers of Key West. While the two factions battle for superiority over the waters, Robert Wagner plays the Greek Romeo who falls for Terry Moore's Key West Juliet.

The competition in the movie is fierce, but it's nothing compared to the real-life war that was being waged at the time between the film industry and television. Determined to distance itself from its upstart rival, the film industry began searching for new technologies. *Beneath the 12 Mile Reef* was only the second film to be shot in the wide-screen CinemaScope process (*The Robe* was the first), and was one of the first to use stereophonic sound.

Although she had been nominated for an Oscar in *Come Back Little Sheba* the year before, Moore is probably best known for her romantic involvements. She claims that during the production of *Reef* she was married to Howard Hughes, a point that has been disputed. But, few will dispute that she is probably the only woman to have been romantically involved with both Hughes and Henry Kissinger.

THE BIG LEAGUER (MGM - 1953)

Melbourne
Written by Herbert Baker
Directed by Robert Aldrich
Starring Edward G. Robinson, Vera-Ellen

The Big Leaguer stars Edward G. Robinson as an aging ballplayer who is given the reins of a youth baseball camp. It was filmed in Melbourne, which was the spring training home of the New York Giants.

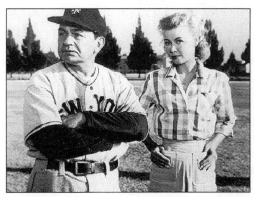

Edward G. Robinson and
Vera-Ellen

While Robinson may seem like an unlikely choice to be cast as a major-league baseball player, he was certainly a hit with the locals. During production, he was so visible at community functions that he was made honorary lifetime vice president of the Chamber of Commerce.

This film was the directorial debut of Robert Aldrich, who would go on to make movies such as *What Ever Happened to Baby Jane, Hush Hush...Sweet Charlotte, The Dirty Dozen* and *The Longest Yard.* Careful viewers will notice Dodger Al Campanis playing himself. Campanis later became famous for racist remarks he made during a broadcast of the news show *Nightline.*

BLACK LIKE ME (Continental - 1964)

Tampa
Written by Gera Lerner, Carl Lerner
Directed by Carl Lerner
Starring James Whitmore

Black Like Me is the adaptation of the famous book by John Howard Griffin. Griffin, a white man, altered his skin pigmentation so that he could see firsthand the inequities faced by blacks in society. (This concept was hilariously parodied years later on NBC's *Saturday Night Live*, when Eddie Murphy did the reverse.)

Griffin was portrayed by character actor James Whitmore, who took the role after numerous leading men declined it fearful of the movie's controversial nature. Producer Julius Tannebaum was responsible for bringing the production (which also shot in New York and Washington D.C.) to Tampa, remembering the area from the time he had served at nearby Drew Air Field. While in Florida, the production shot mostly in the Ybor City section of Tampa.

(See "On Location")

BLACK SUNDAY (Paramount - 1977)

Miami
Written by Ernest Lehman, Kenneth Ross, Ivan Moffat
Directed by John Frankenheimer
Starring Robert Shaw, Marthe Keller, Bruce Dern

"It could be tomorrow."

Paranoia-feeding tag line.

Black Sunday is one of the better examples in a string of disaster movies that cropped up in the mid-'70s. In the film, the terrorist group Black

September plots to hijack the Goodyear blimp over the Orange Bowl, which is packed with fans for the Super Bowl. Robert Shaw plays an Israeli commando and Bruce Dern plays (big surprise) a psychotic Vietnam veteran who is convinced to pilot the blimp.

The film is adapted from the book by Thomas Harris, who also wrote the novel *The Silence of the Lambs*. The most memorable moment of the movie occurs during the finale, when the blimp comes over the edge of the stadium and the fans run in terror.

Poster for *Black Sunday*

The Super Bowl footage was shot during three different trips to the Orange Bowl. The blimp actually did its lurches and dives during a regular season game between the Dolphins and the Colts. The filmmakers returned to the stadium to film footage of Super Bowl X between the Steelers and the Cowboys. Finally, a group of 35,000 movie hopefuls and curious fans braved pouring rain to provide the crowd-reaction shots. (The producers were just about to reschedule shooting when the weather cleared.) Meanwhile, Dolphin great Nat Moore acted as the technical advisor on the field.

Despite the financial benefits to the city—more than $3 million was put into the local economy—Miami was leery of the production. City officials were fearful that, like a Rod Serling film had done for hijacking, the film might inspire real-life terrorists. A group led by Dolphin owner Joe Robbie (who appears in the film as himself) helped convince city officials to reconsider.

Ironically, a similar fear affected a later Florida Super Bowl. While war was being waged in the Persian Gulf, blimps were forbidden to fly over Tampa Stadium during Super Bowl XXV.

(See "On Location")

BLINDFOLD (Universal - 1966)

Ocala
Written by Philip Dunne, W.H. Menger
Directed by Philip Dunne
Starring Rock Hudson, Claudia Cardinale, Alejandro Rey, Jack Warden

In this tongue-in-cheek spy drama, psychiatrist Rock Hudson secretly counsels disturbed but brilliant scientist Alejandro Rey in a Southern swamp. When Rey is kidnapped by spies, Hudson must try to rescue him. In the process, he falls in love with Rey's beautiful sister, played by Claudia Cardinale. The swamp location is Silver Springs, near Ocala.

BLUE CITY (Paramount - 1986)

Florida Keys
Written by Lukas Heller, Walter Hill
Directed by Michelle Manning
Starring Judd Nelson and Ally Sheedy

"It's below Miami and above the law."
Unsuccesful attempt to piggyback on the popularity of Miami Vice.

Blue City almost single-handedly launched and destroyed the career of director Michelle Manning. Fresh from the University of Southern California film school, Manning achieved instant success as the producer of the Brat Pack classic *The Breakfast Club*.

Ready for her directing debut, she passed on the hit film *Pretty in Pink* because she was worried that she might get pigeonholed as a director of women's pictures. Instead, she opted for this action piece with *Breakfast Club* alumni Judd Nelson and Ally Sheedy, and got pigeonholed as a director of bad movies.

Critical reaction was universally negative. *People* magazine summed up its review by quoting a threat from Nelson in the film: "You're going to experience grief and woe of Biblical proportions." He must have seen the dailies.

BODY HEAT (Warner Brothers - 1981)

Lake Worth, Hollywood
Written and Directed by Lawrence Kasdan
Starring William Hurt, Kathleen Turner, Richard Crenna, Ted Danson, Mickey Rourke

"You're not too bright. I like that in a man."
Kathleen Turner delivering a white-hot film debut.

Almost every review, summary and mention of *Body Heat* describes the film as atmospheric. Add this one to the list. The role of the humid South Florida climate is almost as big as those played by William Hurt and Kathleen Turner. Amazingly, the story was originally set in Atlantic City. However, a strike delayed production until winter, and the cold weather drove the filmmakers south.

Kathleen Turner and
William Hurt

The film is an updated version of film noir classics such as *Double Indemnity*. Turner plays the rich wife of Richard Crenna. She convinces lawyer Hurt to murder her husband so that they can run off with all of his money.

Body Heat served as a launching pad for most of the participants. It was the directing debut for Lawrence Kasdan, who had previously written films such as *Raiders of the Lost Ark* and *The Empire Strikes Back*. It also sealed William Hurt's future as one of the pre-eminent leading men of the

American cinema. (Kasdan and Hurt reunited on *The Big Chill* and *The Accidental Tourist*.)

The biggest launch was for former soap actress Turner, who soon climbed up the Hollywood ladder to become the only woman among the top ten box office draws. In this, her film debut, she became an instant icon of sexuality. Barbara Stanwyck said of her performance, "The only one who could have done it better is me."

During production, though, the stars were still unknowns. At one point they had a difficult time getting the proper permits to film on a bridge in nearby Delray Beach. Because of its title, the city leaders thought that the movie was a porno film.

(See "On Location")

BRENDA STARR (Tomorrow Entertainment - 1986)

Jacksonville
Written by James David Buchanan, Jenny Wolkind, Noreen Stone
Directed by Robert Ellis Miller
Starring Brooke Shields, Timothy Dalton

"This is a major feature. We've had TV movies before, but this is for the theater and will probably have international distribution."
The Jacksonville Film Commissioner getting excited. If only she had known....

If *Brenda Starr* were as interesting on screen as it was behind the scenes, it might have played at theaters outside Africa, which for its first six years was the only place the movie had been screened. But 20/20 hindsight offers clues to its ultimate fate.

The announcement of production was big news in Jacksonville. Seventy years after losing the industry to Hollywood, the city was thrilled to get back into big-time filmmaking. Civic boosters were especially proud that the city was selected because of its resemblance (quite mistaken) to 1940s New York, which is the comic strip's setting. (This should have been a clue.)

It was financed by Shiek Abdul Aziz Al-Ibrahim, a brother-in-law of Saudi Arabia's King Fahd. The Shiek's sole instruction was that the title character be played by Brooke Shields, one of his favorite actresses. (Also a clue.)

A rights dispute held up the film's release for years. Apparently, the producers had not bothered to get permission to use the Brenda Starr character. (Curiouser and curiouser.)

A final blow was struck in 1991, just as the film was about to be released. It turned out that its financing was tied to the notorious Bank of Credit and Commerce International. (More oddities than you can shiek a fist at.)

CADDYSHACK (Orion - 1980)

Davie
Written by Brian Doyle-Murray, Harold Ramis, Doug Kenney
Directed by Harold Ramis
Starring Bill Murray, Chevy Chase, Rodney Dangerfield, Ted Knight, Michael O'Keefe

Caddyshack is the type of movie that some people hate to admit they enjoyed. The film's swank country club provides an arena for comedians Rodney Dangerfield, Chevy Chase and Bill Murray to do their stuff without worrying about too much plot getting in the way. Especially memorable is Murray, who solidified his career with his portrayal of Carl, the gopher-hunting groundskeeper.

Davie's Rolling Hills Country Club was selected as the primary location because of its "anywhere" look. Hoping for a hit on the level of *Animal House*, Orion hired *House* veterans Doug Kenney and Harold Ramis to write, produce and direct the film. But,

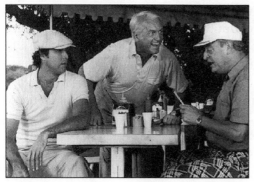

Chevy Chase, Ted Knight and Rodney Dangerfield

during production, word started coming back to the studio that there was a big cocaine problem on the film. At the center of the controversy was National Lampoon co-founder Kenney, who died a year later at the age of thirty-three.

The film was not well-received critically, and even director Ramis referred to it as a "six-million-dollar scholarship to film school." Still, audiences loved it, and the box office was good enough to lead to *Caddyshack II*, which also was filmed in Davie. (See "On Location")

CAPE FEAR (Universal - 1991)

Fort Lauderdale, Hollywood
Written by Wesley Strick
Directed by Martin Scorsese
Starring Robert DeNiro, Nick Nolte, Jessica Lange, Juliette Lewis

"Come out, come out, wherever you are."
A deranged Robert De Niro to a very frightened Nick Nolte.

He may have had difficulties in Hollywood, California, but New York-based director Martin Scorsese has nothing but fans in Hollywood, Florida, which provided many locations for his film *Cape Fear*. Unable to give him an Oscar, city officials did the next best thing and presented him with the key to the city. (Would you trust the director of *Taxi Driver* with the key to anything?)

At first, Scorsese was reluctant to direct this remake of the 1962 Gregory Peck/Robert Mitchum thriller of the same name. He agreed only after repeated requests from Robert De Niro and Steven Spielberg, who was originally slated to direct. Spielberg's Amblin' Entertainment also produced the film.

De Niro received a well-deserved Oscar nomination

for his portrayal of ex-con Max Cady, who exacts revenge on Nick Nolte, the lawyer who did a bad job defending him at his trial. But, the movie is stolen by newcomer Juliette Lewis, who also got an Oscar nomination for her role as Nolte's daughter.

Rather than borrowing, the film tips its hat to the original. It features a reorchestration of Bernard Hermann's score and cameo appearances by Peck and Mitchum. But Scorsese puts his own spin on things. Primarily, he replaces the idyllic family of the original film with one that hides a closet full of secrets and strained relationships.

Relations were sometimes strained

Robert DeNiro, Jessica Lange and Nick Nolte

between the filmmakers and Hollywood merchants worried about lost business. As is typical in these types of disputes, it was nothing that a few movie stars and a little bit of money couldn't clear up. Filming took place all over Broward County. The studios at Fort Lauderdale Production Central were left with a special water stage that was constructed for the film's finale.

(See "On Location")

CEASE FIRE (Double Helix - 1985)

Miami
Written by George Fernandez
Directed by David Nutter
Starring Don Johnson, Lisa Blount, Robert Lyons

Most people have seen Don Johnson, as Sonny Crockett, battle drug lords to save the streets of Miami. But before he made it big on television, he fought haunting memories of Vietnam to save his marriage in the low-budget film *Cease Fire*. Since Ricardo Tubbs wasn't around for support, he opted for group therapy at the local vet center. Many of the production personnel were recent University of Miami film-school graduates, some of whom followed Johnson to *Miami Vice* a few years later.

THE CHAMP (MGM - 1979)

Hialeah
Written by Walter Newman
Directed by Franco Zeffirelli
Starring Jon Voight, Faye Dunaway, Ricky Schroder, Jack Warden

"The more you love, the harder you fight."

Poster advertisement.

The Best Picture Oscar for 1979 went to *Kramer vs. Kramer*, for its story of a man fighting his ex-wife to keep custody of his son. Meanwhile, huge box-office receipts went to *Rocky II* for its story of a boxer coming out of retirement and risking his

life for one last fight. That same year, *The Champ* starred Jon Voight as a down and out boxer who fights his ex-wife to keep custody of his son and has to come out of retirement to risk his life for one last fight. It's like *deja vu* all over again.

It especially seems familiar when you consider that the

Ricky Schroder, Jon Voight and Jack Warden

movie is the second remake of the 1931 Wallace Beery film. (The first remake was *The Clown* starring Red Skelton.) Ricky Schroder plays the idolizing son and looks much more like Jon Voight than *Kramer's*

Justin Henry looks like Dustin Hoffman. Faye Dunaway is the ice princess ex-wife whom the audience loves to hate.

Much of the film was shot at the Hialeah racetrack, where Voight spends too much time gambling and not enough with Schroder. One of the more difficult scenes to coordinate called for a large crowd of extras to come to the track dressed in pink.

Zeffirelli, who had already directed *Romeo and Juliet* and television's *Jesus of Nazareth*, contrasts the lushness of Dunaway's world with the grittiness of Voight's to reach for every tear-provoking moment. Voight had recently returned from a four-year acting hiatus to star in the previous year's *Coming Home*, which earned him an Oscar for Best Actor.

(See "On Location")

CHINA MOON (Orion - 1992)

Lakeland
Written by Roy Carlson
Directed by John Bailey
Starring Ed Harris, Madeleine Stowe, Charles Dance

"Every time I got a little bit uncomfortable, or cold, or wet, I'd think of *The Abyss* and say this is just fine."

Ed Harris happy to be on land again.

After the notoriously difficult underwater production of *The Abyss*, Ed Harris was glad to play a small-town detective in *China Moon*. In the story, Harris falls in love with Madeleine Stowe, the wife of a rich banker played by Charles Dance. When Dance is murdered, the investigation leads back to Harris.

The film was written specifically for the Lakeland area and was the second feature produced by Kevin Costner's Tig Productions. (*Dances with Wolves* was the first.) Nine weeks were spent filming around Polk County, with most interiors being shot at a makeshift studio inside an abandoned stuffed-animal warehouse. It is the directorial debut of John Bailey, whose credits as a cinematographer include *The Accidental Tourist* and *The Big Chill*.

(See "On Location")

CLAMBAKE (United Artists - 1967)

Miami
Written by Arthur Browne, Jr.
Directed by Arthur Nadel
Starring Elvis Presley, Shelley Fabares, Bill Bixby, Gary Merrill

If nothing else, *Clambake* has the coolest title of any Elvis movie. In this one, he stars as an oil heir desperate to find a girl that loves him and not his money. He becomes a water-ski instructor and fights Bill Bixby for the affection of frequent co-star Shelley Fabares.

Elvis and friends

Clambake had none of the controversy that dogged the production of *Follow That Dream* five years earlier in Yankeetown. Miami gets good publicity, and the grand finale takes place during the Orange Bowl Regatta in the Miami Marine Stadium. The King even does Mother Nature one better when he stands on a causeway and points to a mountain. (Don Johnson could never have made a mountain in Miami.)

COCOON (20th Century-Fox - 1985)

St. Petersburg
Written by Tom Benedek
Directed by Ron Howard
Starring Don Ameche, Wilford Brimley, Hume Cronyn, Brian Dennehey, Jack Gilford, Steve Guttenberg, Maureen Stapleton, Jessica Tandy

"If this is foreplay, I'm a dead man."

Steve Guttenberg experiencing extraterrestial lovemaking for the first time.

ocoon proves William Goldman's oft-quoted statement that "Nobody knows anything" when it comes to predicting what movie audiences will like. According to conventional wisdom, the elderly cast should have driven away the teenage viewers

Wilford Brimley and
Maureen Stapleton

faster than a National Geographic documentary. Likewise, the science fiction/fantasy elements should have sent their parents packing right behind them. Defying such logic, *Cocoon* went on to please audiences and critics, and to show that *Splash* was no fluke for director Ron Howard.

In the movie, a group of St. Petersburg senior citizens discovers a fountain of youth in a swimming pool near their retirement home. It turns out that the pool has been supplied with a life force by space aliens. The movie unfolds to tell a story about life, death and the eldery, whom society has cast as aliens here on earth.

In an outstanding cast, Don Ameche manages to steal the show, breakdancing along the way, to deliver a perfomance that won a well-deserved Oscar for Best Supporting Actor. The day after the award show, nearly every newspaper in America carried a picture of him clutching the statuette. The attention was not so much to honor his distinguished career as it was because of the outfit worn by presenter Cher. She donned a dramatic two-piece gown and headdress to steal a little attention for herself.

Although *Cocoon* solidified Howard's directing career, it almost marked the career end for Robert Zemeckis, who was originally slated to direct the movie. He was fired from the project when Fox executives were less than thrilled with his direction of *Romancing the Stone*. Once again, Goldman's statement proved true, as *Romancing the Stone* packed theaters all summer. The following year, *Cocoon*'s unexpected success was overshadowed by the surprise hit of that year, *Back to the Future*, which just happened to be co-written and directed by—you guessed it—Robert Zemeckis.

(See "On Location")

COCOON: THE RETURN (20th Century-Fox - 1988)

Miami
Written by Stephen McPherson
Directed by Daniel Petrie
Starring Don Ameche, Wilford Brimley, Hume Cronyn, Brian Dennehey, Jack Gilford, Steve Guttenberg, Maureen Stapleton, Jessica Tandy

While *Cocoon*'s success may have been unpredictable, a sequel was inevitable. Not only does *Cocoon: The Return* bring back all of the cast members, it borrows most of the plot from the first one as well: Everyone has to decide between eternal life on Anterea or mortal life with family members back on Earth. In fact, the only real difference between the two is that the second was filmed in Miami instead of St. Petersburg.

COUPE DE VILLE (Universal - 1990)

St. Petersburg, Miami
Written by Mike Binder
Directed by Joe Roth
Starring Daniel Stern, Patrick Dempsey, Arye Gross, Annabeth Gish, Alan Arkin

It's 1963, and a trio of brothers has to drive a car from Detroit to Miami in time for their father's birthday. On the way they fight, they bond and they debate the lyrics of the song "Louie Louie."

One begins to wonder how long Daniel Stern can continue to ride the classic rock-and-roll, coming-of-age, male-bonding wave that has carried his career for so long. It began with 1979's *Breaking Away*, continued through *Diner* in 1982 and on to 1991's *City Slickers*. He even provides the adult Kevin's voice-over for the television show *The Wonder Years*.

CREATURE FROM THE BLACK LAGOON (Universal - 1954)

Wakulla Springs, Ocala
Written by Harry Essex and Arthur Ross
Directed by Jack Arnold
Starring Richard Carlson, Julie Adams, Ben Chapman, Ricou Browning

Terrifying Monster of the ages raging with pent-up passions! ...with every man his mortal enemy ...and a woman's beauty his prey!

Poster advertisement.

In 1954 Universal, which had previously brought *Frankenstein*, *Dracula* and a host of other horror movies to the screen, pulled out all the stops to promote its newest monster: the *Creature from the Black Lagoon*. Nothing was too horrific for *Creature*'s ad campaign. Even the novelty of 3-D wasn't special enough; the process was dubbed Thrill Wonder 3-D Horrorscope.

The story surrounds a group of scientists who travel up the Amazon and discover a creature that is half man and half fish. While the plot may be standard, great care was taken to design the creature. Initial sketches of the gill man were modeled after the Academy Award statuette. A make-up bust of actress Ann Sheridan was used as a base upon which to sculpt its facial features with modeling clay. More than $12,000 later, the studio decided that the Creature was ready, and the project was greenlighted.

The Creature

Unlike *Dracula's* Bela Lugosi and Boris Karloff's monster in *Frankenstein*, the actor portraying the gill man has his face obscured by the costume. This allowed the studio to specialize, casting two actors for the part. Brawny U.S. Marine Ben Chapman played the creature on land, while the smaller Ricou Browning played the creature underwater. The two gill-man suits were made to such specifications that only Chapman and Browning could wear them. Browning's was a lighter color so that it was more visible in the dark water.

The fact that Browning, a swimming champion, was able to hold his breath for up to four minutes made him a natural for the role. He is credited with creating the ungainly, torso-twisting "creature swimming technique" that has been a hallmark of underwater horror films ever since.

In the end, all this attention to detail proved worthwhile. Filmed in Wakulla Springs and Silver Springs, the film grossed $3,000,000, spawned two sequels and helped save the studio from impending bankruptcy.

The film secured a lasting place in film history the following year thanks to the Marilyn Monroe film *The Seven Year Itch*. During the famed scene in which

Marilyn's skirt is blown up as she stands over a vent, she is in front of Manhattan's Trans-Lux Theatre, which displays a marquee promoting *Creature*.

(See: "On Location")

CRISSCROSS (MGM/Pathe - 1992)

Key West
Written by Scott Sommer
Directed by Chris Menges
Starring Goldie Hawn, Arliss Howard

Set in Key West circa 1969, *CrissCross* stars Goldie Hawn as a single mother who becomes a stripper to help provide for her son. When he learns of this, he starts dealing in the area's active drug culture, determined to make enough money so that she can quit. Stories have circulated that the film was saddled with that common Hollywood ailment "creative differences." Originally focused on the son, the script was changed to feature Hawn's role and offer a more upbeat tone.

CROSS CREEK (EMI - 1983)

Hawthorne, Micanopy
Written by Dalene Young
Directed by Martin Ritt
Starring Mary Steenburgen, Rip Torn, Peter Coyote, Alfre Woodard

"The true story of the woman who wrote *The Yearling*."

Less-than-engaging selling line.

Cross Creek is based on Marjorie Kinnan Rawlings' autobiography. A New Yorker, she moves to the backwoods of Florida intent on writing gothic novels. Instead, she finds herself entranced by the area and its people. The relationship between her neighbor Rip Torn and his daughter inspires her to

write the endearing classic *The Yearling*. She also finds love in the arms of Norton Baskin, played by Peter Coyote.

Production took place in actual Rawlings country, in and around Hawthorne. Like Rawlings, Torn was taken by the area, and while the rest of the cast and crew stayed in Ocala, he stayed closer to allow

Rip Torn and
Mary Steenburgen

himself time for fishing. He was nominated for an Academy Award, as was Alfre Woodard, who plays Rawling's maid Geeche. Look for Steenburgen's real-life husband Malcolm McDowell as famed literary agent Maxwell Perkins, and Rawlings' real-life husband Norton Baskin in a cameo as a man giving her directions.

(See: "On Location")

CROSSWINDS (Paramount - 1951)

Homosassa Springs
Written and Directed by Lewis Foster
Starring John Payne, Rhonda Fleming, Forrest Tucker

In *Crosswinds*, Florida doubles for New Guinea, where John Payne has to battle headhunters and pirates while searching for gold lost in an airplane crash. It's the type of adventure movie to which Steven Spielberg paid homage with the Indiana Jones series. Writer/director Lewis Foster also wrote the book *The Gentleman from Montana*, which was the basis for the film classic *Mr. Smith Goes to Washington*.

CUBA CROSSING (Key West - 1980)

Key West
Written and Directed by Chuck Workman
Starring Stuart Whitman, Robert Vaughn

Key West mayor/bartender/soldier-of-fortune Tony Terracino is the main character in *Cuba Crossing*. In the movie, Terracino, played by Stuart Whitman, is involved in a plot to overthrow Castro. Writer/director Chuck Workman later went on to win an Academy Award for *Precious Images*, a documentary made up of famous scenes and moments from classic movies. Those interested in the real-life Terracino should go to his famous bar, Captain Tony's, or listen to Jimmy Buffet's song "Last Mango in Paris."
(See "On Location")

D.A.R.Y.L. (Paramount - 1985)

Orlando
Written by David Ambrose
Directed by Simon Wincer
Starring Michael McKean, Mary Beth Hurt, Barrett Oliver

Data Analyzing Robot Youth Lifeform
The meaning of the title's acronym.

D.A.R.Y.L. is a sweet movie that not many people went to see. Barrett Oliver stars as a Pentagon-created boy named Daryl—sort of a sci-fi version of *Pinocchio*. However, he has no idea where he comes from and is placed in the care of loving foster parents Mary Beth Hurt and Michael McKean. Only later, when the Pentagon comes back to get him, do his special skills make sense.

This film marked the beginning of Orlando's recent emergence as a production center.

(See "On Location")

THE DAY OF THE DOLPHIN (Avco Embassy - 1973)

Miami
Written by Buck Henry
Directed by Mike Nichols
Starring George C. Scott

If *Flipper* and *Black Sunday* were to play in a triple feature, *The Day of the Dolphin* would have to be the movie that plays between them. The story concerns a plot to use dolphins to attach a bomb to the hull of the President's yacht. George C. Scott plays a good-guy researcher. He talks to the dolphins and they talk back in Buck Henry's voice.

Although screenwriter Henry and director Mike Nichols had better results with satire, as in *The Graduate* and *Catch-22*, *The Day of the Dolphin* was able to pull a few tears out of a large portion of the audience.

DAYS OF THUNDER (Paramount - 1990)

Daytona
Written by Robert Towne
Directed by Tony Scott
Starring Tom Cruise, Robert Duvall, Nicole Kidman, Randy Quaid

"Cruise like Thunder."

Poster advertisement.

It's hard to call a film that grossed $84,000,000 a failure, but to many that's what *Days of Thunder* became. The film reunited *Top Gun* alumni Tom

Cruise, director Tony Scott and producers Don Simpson and Jerry Bruckheimer. With Oscar winners Robert Duvall and Robert Towne added to the formula, Paramount was certain it had a hit.

Cruise stars as a driver on the NASCAR racing circuit bent on winning the Daytona 500. Daytona was eager to host the big-budget feature and bent over backward to help production. The city even closed off a stretch of beach for the filming of a race on the sand. Meanwhile, NASCAR saw the film as a vehicle to increase its following, and allowed two cars from Hendrick Motorsports, with cameras mounted, to run in the first forty laps of the actual race.

Tom Cruise

While the filmmakers dismissed claims that the film was merely *Top Gun* on wheels, they were banking on a top-gun performance at the theaters, with box-office predictions in the hundreds of millions. Paramount chose this time to announce a "visionary alliance" with the producing team of Simpson and Bruckheimer. This one-of-a-kind deal guaranteed the pair unprecendented creative and financial control on future films.

The production was much like the race cars it glorified—slick, fast and seemingly unbeatable. But a funny thing happened on the way to the finish line: *Thunder* borrowed a page from its own script; the engine sputtered and the drivers lost control.

Rumors circulated that the script never came together, and had the budget spiraling out of control around $60 million. Meanwhile, tabloids were awash with stories that Cruise's marriage to actress Mimi Rogers was on the rocks. All of the rumors were denied. All of them were true.

Paramount rushed the team toward a May deadline to take full advantage of the summer movie season. The film opened to big box office, but never performed as well as expected.

Paramount hinted that Simpson and Bruckheimer had doomed the picture by overspending. The producers said that the studio rushed the film into release before it could be properly finished. The "visionary alliance" disappeared and the producers left the studio. The only one who came out ahead was Cruise, who married co-star Kidman.

(See "On Location")

DEEP THROAT (Arrow - 1972)

Miami, Fort Lauderdale
Written and directed by Gerard Damiano
Starring Linda Lovelace

Although you won't find it in many Film Bureau lists, the porno classic *Deep Throat* has earned over $300,000,000, making it the highest-grossing film in Florida's history. The film was produced by Gerard Damiano in six days, at a total cost of $24,000. Its notoriety only increased when star Linda Lovelace claimed that she had performed under threats of violence. The movie's title was adopted as the cover name for Bob Woodward's Watergate informant, made famous by *All the President's Men*.

DISTANT DRUMS (Warner Brothers - 1951)

Naples, St. Augustine, Ocala
Written by Niven Busch, Martin Rackin
Directed by Raoul Walsh
Starring Gary Cooper

Objective Everglades! could have been the title of the Gary Cooper movie *Distant Drums*. The film is a remake of the war classic *Objective Burma!*, which was also directed by Raoul Walsh. Cooper plays the leader of a military expedition that is driven deep into the Everglades by hostile Seminole Indians.

According to Walsh, Cooper was unhappy during production. "We were working in the Everglades, plagued with snakes and mosquitoes. Coop was unhappy and short-tempered in general. He killed a rattler and tore off the skin like a banana peel." As it turns out, Cooper was still in Florida when his impending divorce was announced and rumors of his affair with actress Patricia Neal reached a climax.

(See "On Location")

DOC HOLLYWOOD (Warner Brothers - 1991)

Micanopy, Gainesville
Written by Daniel Pyne
Directed by Michael Caton-Jones
Starring Michael J. Fox, Julie Warner, Woody Harrelson, David Ogden Stiers, Bridgette Fonda, Jasmine the Pig

**"He's a big city plastic surgeon...
In a small town that doesn't take plastic."**

Cute ad line, like the movie.

Doc Hollywood is the first American film by Scottish director Michael Caton-Jones. The romantic comedy stars Michael J. Fox as a plastic surgeon en route to Beverly Hills when his car breaks down in Grady, South Carolina—Squash Capital of the South. Newcomer Julie Warner plays the reason Fox might not go to Hollywood after all.

During production, a mini-war broke out between the filmmakers and a local

Michael J. Fox

antique dealer. Unhappy with the production, she hung a giant banner reading "Micanopy Antiques" in front of her store. The city quickly passed a special town ordinance prohibiting obstruction with filming.

Still, the cast and crew won over the community, and helped out more than the local economy. They raised a few thousand dollars for the homeless and helped out in a soup kitchen. At a University of Florida performance of *Peter and the Wolf*, Fox was a surprise narrator, and co-star David Ogden Stiers conducted the orchestra.

(See: "On Location")

DON'T DRINK THE WATER (Avco Embassy - 1969)

Miami
Written by R.S. Allen, Harvey Bullock
Directed by Howard Morris
Starring Jackie Gleason, Estelle Parsons

Why did *Don't Drink the Water* film in Miami? It wasn't because of the scenery—the comedy is set in the oppressive Eastern-bloc "nation" of Vulgaria. It wasn't because of the weather—almost all of the movie takes place inside the American Embassy. It wasn't even because of the area's talent pool. Almost everyone involved came in from New York and Los Angeles. Everyone, that is, except for Jackie Gleason.

If you can't move Jackie to the production, you move the production to Jackie, and Jackie didn't like to leave Miami. The networks built him a television studio in town, so it only made sense that the movies come to him as well.

Based on a play by Woody Allen, the movie stars Gleason as a caterer who is mistaken for a spy behind the Iron Curtain. Along with wife Estelle

Parsons and daughter Joan Delaney, he must take asylum inside the American Embassy.

It's not at all surprising that there's a television feel to the comedy. All the principals began on the small screen. Gleason was the star of *The Honeymooners* and *The Jackie Gleason Show*. Director Howard Morris and Woody Allen both began their careers on *Your Show of Shows*, and screenwriters R.S. Allen and Harvey Bullock did most of their writing for Hanna-Barbera cartoons.

EASY TO LOVE (MGM - 1953)

Cypress Gardens
Written by Laslo Vadnay, William Roberts
Directed by Charles Walters
Starring Esther Williams, Tony Martin, Van Johnson

"Wet she's a star. Dry she ain't."

Producer's description of oft-wet actress Esther Williams.

When she started at MGM, Esther Williams began the normal pattern the studio used to groom its young stars. She played small parts in *Andy Hardy's Double Life* and *A Guy Named Joe*. But her third film, *Bathing Beauty*, changed everything. The former swimming champion began a long string of Technicolor escapist fare that featured her in a bathing suit leading huge production numbers.

The trick to making these movies was coming up with a plot that let Williams slip into some swimwear and hit the water. In *Easy to Love*, the writers gave up and made her the star of an

Esther Williams

aqua-show. She is in love with her boss Van Johnson, but he doesn't notice her until she starts to romance crooner Tony Martin.

The most notable features of the film are choreographer Busby Berkeley's fantastic production numbers, including a giant water-ski finale. Berkeley worked on only two more movies after *Easy to Love*, and the numbers here are considered the last great examples of his style.

(See "On Location")

EDWARD SCISSORHANDS (20th Century-Fox - 1990)

Wesley Chapel
Written by Caroline Thompson
Directed by Tim Burton
Starring Johnny Depp, Winona Ryder, Dianne Wiest, Alan Arkin, Vincent Price, Kathy Baker, Anthony Michael Hall

"I love the skies here. You have nice big white clouds."
Director Tim Burton explaining why he decided to film in Florida.

Johnny Depp

In the film *Edward Scissorhands*, Edward is the creation of childless inventor Vincent Price. Unfortunately, Price dies before completing him, and Edward is left human in every way except for one: He has only scissors for hands, a fact that forever makes him an outcast in society. The film is said to be the most personal for director Tim Burton, which has to make you wonder about him. (After all, his first film was a short called *Frankenweenie*.)

Hot off of the mega-success of *Batman*, Burton scouted countless subdivisions in Florida and Texas looking for a perfectly anonymous tract-housing neighborhood. He finally selected the Carpenter's Run subdivision outside Wesley Chapel, north of Tampa. The film was to be an all-Florida production, with stage work set to take place at Universal Studios Florida. But there were scheduling conflicts with the sound stages, and the production team went back to Hollywood to wrap shooting.

Many people, including Tom Cruise, were rumored to be in the running for the lead part, which went to Florida native Johnny Depp. Depp's on-screen love interest was played by his real-life fiancee Winona Ryder.

(See "On Location")

ERNEST SAVES CHRISTMAS (Touchstone - 1988)

Orlando
Written by B. Kline, Ed Turner
Directed by John Cherry
Starring Jim Varney

Jim Varney has made a career out of the goofy camera-mugging character Ernest P. Worrell. After hitting it big with commercials, he moved to the big screen to make the Ernest trilogy. Most critics hate the films, but they offer harmless entertainment for children. Still, the series seems to be running its course as the movies get progressively shorter, with the third installment, *Ernest Goes to Jail*, coming in at only 81 minutes long. The second of the three films, *Ernest Saves Christmas* was filmed almost entirely in Orlando and at the Disney/MGM Studios.

(See: "On Location")

Jim Varney and Santa

FAT SPY (Magna – 1966)

Cape Coral
Written by Matthew Andrews
Directed by Joseph Cates
Starring Phyllis Diller, Jack E. Leonard, Brian Donlevy, Jayne Mansfield

Much like Roseanne Barr, Phyllis Diller was already a working mother when she hit it big doing a comedy routine skewering her family and herself. She began a career in movies and often appeared opposite Bob Hope. In *Fat Spy*, she joins Jack E. Leonard, Brian Donlevy and Jayne Mansfield in a search for the Fountain of Youth on a small Florida island.

FIRES WITHIN (MGM/Pathe – 1991)

Miami
Written by Cynthia Cidre
Directed by Gillian Armstrong
Starring Jimmy Smits, Greta Scacchi, Vincent D'Onofrio

A film that got lost somewhere between production and distribution, *Fires Within* was directed by Australian Gillian Armstrong and is set in Miami's Little Havana. (*Little Havana* was the original title.) After years in one of Castro's prisons, Jimmy Smits makes it to Florida, only to find that his wife Greta Scacchi has fallen in love with an American fisherman, played by Vincent D'Onofrio. The Calle Ocho Festival had to be recreated during production. In real life, Scacchi and D'Onofrio did begin a romance.

A FLASH OF GREEN (Spectrafilm - 1984)

Sarasota, Bradenton, Venice, Fort Myers
Written and Directed by Victor Nuñez
Starring Ed Harris, Blair Brown, Richard Jordan

"He's unhappy with what Hollywood has done with his stories in the past and he's willing to give a crazy independent filmmaker a chance."
Victor Nuñez explaining why Florida writer John D. MacDonald, best known for his Travis McGee novels, let him try his hand at the film version of A Flash of Green.

A number of different Gulf Coast communities make up the movie's fictional Palm City. Ed Harris plays a journalist who turns his back on a local environmental group. Real-life husband and wife Richard Jordan and Blair Brown star as a corrupt county commisioner and the leader of a conservation group. Jordan also produced the film.

Like he had done previously on *Gal Young Un*, Nuñez did almost everything but write the music and act. To finance the film, he went to a number of sources. In the end the $800,000 budget came from a mix of investors and the Public Television Playhouse, as well as grants from the National Endowment for the Arts and the Rockefeller Foundation.

Like many writers, Nuñez is determined to work regionally, which is why he has resisted the temptation to leave Florida for the bigger budgets of Hollywood. Apparently, the small scale didn't phase Harris, who lists *A Flash of Green* as his personal favorite among his films.

FLIGHT OF THE NAVIGATOR (Disney - 1986)

Fort Lauderdale
Written by Michael Burton, Matt MacManus
Directed by Randal Kleiser
Starring Joey Cramer, Veronica Cartwright, Sarah Jessica Parker

More family entertainment from the director of *Grease* and *The Blue Lagoon*. *Flight of the Navigator* is the story of a boy's adventure on a flying saucer. As in most post-E.T. science-fiction stories, the rules are simple: Aliens and kids are good; adults and the government are bad.

FLIPPER (MGM - 1963)

Miami
Written by Arthur Weiss
Directed by James B. Clark
Starring Chuck Connors, Luke Halpin, Mitzi the Dolphin

Hungarian emigre Ivan Tors made family entertainment and the animal kingdom his life's purpose (or is it porpoise?). Responsible for films

Luke Halpin and Flipper

and television shows such as *Gentle Ben* and *Clarence the Cross-eyed Lion*, he is best known for *Flipper*, the story of boy gets dolphin, boy loses dolphin, dolphin saves boy from killer sharks.

The screenplay was based on a story by Tors studio executive Ricou Browning, who got his start in movies in costume as *The Creature from the Black Lagoon*. *Flipper* spawned a sequel (*Flipper's New Adventure*) and a television series. A remake is scheduled to be shot in the Keys and at the Disney/MGM Studios.

FOLKS (PentAmerica - 1992)

Briny Breezes, Boca Raton
Written by Robert Klane
Directed by Ted Kotcheff
Starring Tom Selleck, Don Ameche, Anne Jackson

olks is a black comedy about Alzheimer's disease. Tom Selleck plays a down-on-his-luck stockbroker whose parents, Don Ameche and Anne Jackson, offer to kill themselves so that he can start over with their insurance money.

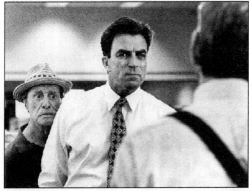

Don Ameche and Tom Selleck

The production spent five weeks in Florida. In the process, it commandeered Briny Breezes, a trailer-park hamlet near Boynton Beach. At Briny Breezes, the film company removed a house from its foundation and replaced it with one that could be burned in the film.

The principals had all worked in Florida before. Ameche won an Oscar for his role in *Cocoon*, Selleck was an executive producer of the Burt Reynolds TV series *B. L. Stryker* and Kotcheff directed some shots in South Florida for the Burt Reynolds movie *Switching Channels*.

(See "On Location")

FOLLOW THAT DREAM (United Artists - 1962)

Yankeetown, Ocala
Written by Charles Lederer
Directed by Gordon Douglas
Starring Elvis Presley, Arthur O'Connell

In 1962, Elvis descended on Central Florida to make the movie *Follow That Dream*. The story concerns a group of squatters who stake out some waterfront land. A public stir erupted when it was learned that the Florida Development Commission had given the producers $8,000 to help offset production costs.

The public was probably just miffed that the King was inaccesible during production. Colonel Tom Parker ran tight security and immediately after shooting, Presley would disappear into his air-conditioned Cadillac and drive off to the posh Port Paradise Hotel.

At least one area resident was inspired by the filming. Gainesville native Tom Petty claims that he was first compelled to become a musician at the age of seven, when he watched Elvis working on the movie.

GAL YOUNG UN (Nuñez Films - 1979)

Gainesville
Written and Directed by Victor Nuñez
Starring Dana Preu, David Peck

"It's hard because you want to pay people better."
Victor Nuñez on the difficulties of independent filmmaking.

Based on a story by Marjorie Kinnan Rawlings, *Gal Young Un* is an example of independent filmmaking in its truest sense. Not only did Victor Nuñez write and direct the movie, he was also the film's producer, cinematographer, editor and distributor.

Most of the film's $94,000 budget came via grants from the National Endowment for the Humanities and the Florida Fine Arts Council. The lead was played by a professor from Florida A&M University. Almost all of the shooting took place on weekends because cast members couldn't interrupt their full-time jobs. The film overcame its humble beginnings to win praise and awards at the New York, Chicago and Cannes film festivals. It put Nuñez in a position to direct the screen adaptation of John B. MacDonald's *A Flash of Green*.

GHOST STORY (Universal - 1981)

DeLand
Written by Lawrence Cohen
Directed by John Irvin
Starring Fred Astaire, Melvyn Douglas, Douglas Fairbanks Jr., John Houseman

Like *Cocoon*, *Ghost Story* stars a group of older actors whose talents are too often ignored in Hollywood. Unlike *Cocoon*, this film does it poorly. The story concerns a quartet of old men who get together and tell each other ghost stories. Part of it was filmed in DeLand at Stetson University's Elizabeth Hall.

GIRL HAPPY (MGM - 1965)

Fort Lauderdale
Written by Harvey Bullock, R.S. Allen
Directed by Boris Sagal
Starring Elvis Presley, Shelley Fabares, Jackie Coogan

He may have driven a Cadillac, but the true Elvis "vehicle" is a movie with a loose plot that lets him sing, dance and hang out with girls in bathing suits. Not to be confused with the Elvis movie *Girls! Girls! Girls!*, *Girl Happy* is one such vehicle. Set in Fort Lauderdale during spring break, the King plays the leader of a rock-and-roll band that is hired by a gangster to play at his nightclub. Part of the deal is that he must also look after the gangster's daughter, Shelley Fabares.

Like many of the MGM films in Florida, it was produced by Joe Pasternak, who had helped create the Fort Lauderdale spring break craze five years earlier with *Where the Boys Are*. Songs include "Spring Fever," "Do the Clam" and the improbably titled "Fort Lauderdale Chamber of Commerce."

THE GODFATHER, PART II (Paramount - 1974)

Miami
Written by Francis Ford Coppola, Mario Puzo
Directed by Francis Ford Coppola
Starring Al Pacino, Lee Strasberg

Considering that *The Godfather, Part II* runs 3 hours and 20 minutes, Miami's role can only be considered a cameo. But, when a film wins Best Picture, you take what you can get.

In the film, Al Pacino plays Michael Corleone, who visits the North Miami home of mafia financier Hyman Roth, played by Lee Strasberg. The film returns to Miami during the climax, when Roth is assasinated at the International Airport.

This was the film debut for famed acting teacher Strasberg, who was nominated for a Best Supporting Actor Oscar. Ironically, he lost out to former student Robert De Niro, who played the young Vito Corleone in the movie. Pacino later returned to Miami to portray another mobster, Tony Montana, in *Scarface*. Although they didn't shoot him in the airport, the press did manage to drive him out of town.

GOLDFINGER (MGM - 1964)

Miami Beach
Written by Richard Maibaum, Paul Dehn
Directed by Guy Hamilton
Starring Sean Connery, Shirley Eaton

"I might have known that M wouldn't have booked me into the best hotel on Miami Beach out of gratitude."

James Bond plugging the Fountainebleu.

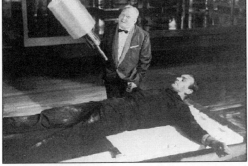

Sean Connery and Gert Fröbe

Beach. Miami Beach. After the standard credit sequence and an opening chase, a sexy overhead view of Miami Beach at its peak begins the best of all James Bond films.

The Miami scenes are set at the famed Fountainebleu Hotel. This is where Bond girl Shirley Eaton is asphyxiated with molten gold.

Unfortunately, Sean Connery was busy filming *Marnie* with Alfred Hitchcock, and had to do his parts of the scenes in a studio in England.
(See "On Location")

THE GREATEST (Columbia - 1977)

Miami
Written by Ring Lardner, Jr.
Directed by Tom Gries
Starring Muhammad Ali, Ernest Borgnine, Robert Duvall, James Earl Jones, Paul Winfield

Some of this biography of Muhammad Ali was filmed in Miami, where Ali trainer Angelo Dundee had a gym. James Earl Jones plays

Muhammad Ali

Malcom X, who converts Cassius Clay to Islam in a Miami storefront mosque. There is a certain symmetry to this, because in *Roots: The Next Generation* Jones plays Alex Haley, and Haley wrote *The Autobiography of Malcolm X*.

In making the movie, Ali was determined to offer a family entertainment antidote to the Mandingo movies starring rival boxer Ken Norton. The theme song, "The Greatest Love," was later made into a hit record by Whitney Houston, who sang it to Ali at a celebrity gala honoring his 50th birthday.

THE GREATEST SHOW ON EARTH (Paramount - 1952)

Sarasota
Written by Fredrick Frank, Theodore St. John, Frank Cavett, Barre Lyndon
Directed by Cecil B. DeMille
Starring Betty Hutton, James Stewart, Charlton Heston, Dorothy Lamour, Emmett Kelly

Cecil B. De Mille meets P.T. Barnum: It's a match made in spectacle heaven. De Mille made his 69th film with this dramatized version of the Ringling Brothers, Barnum and Bailey Circus. Production took place at the circus's Florida headquarters in Sarasota and starred a relatively unknown Charlton Heston.

De Mille spent years planning the production. Paramount paid $250,000 to use Ringling's facilities and the slogan The Greatest Show on Earth. When he heard of the project, Jimmy Stewart sent the director a telegram asking to play the part of a clown, and two days later got an offer to be in the movie.

De Mille was demanding of his actors and required that they be able to perform all their own routines in the movie. This meant that Betty Hutton had to learn the trapeze, and Gloria Graham had to let an elephant rest his foot just above her face. During production, Cornel Wilde discovered that he had a fear of heights. De Mille teased him continually. One day when Wilde was putting on some clogs, the director said, "Better not wear those, Mr. Wilde. You're afraid of heights."

Emmett Kelly, Betty Hutton and James Stewart

The film was a surprise winner of the Oscar for Best Picture, beating out favorite *High Noon*. The reason can be tied to the McCarythism of the day. *High Noon* and its screenwriter, Carl Foreman, were considered subversive and communistic. To top it off, powerful columnist Hedda Hopper had launched an all-out campaign against the Western, and *Greatest* won as a result.

A GUY NAMED JOE (MGM - 1944)

Tampa
Written by Dalton Trumbo
Directed by Victor Fleming
Starring Spencer Tracy, Irene Dunne, Van Johnson

In *A Guy Named Joe*, Spencer Tracy plays a wartime pilot who dies and becomes the guardian angel to a younger pilot, played by Van Johnson. The situation is complicated when Johnson falls for Irene Dunne, who had been Tracy's girlfriend. Some of the film's military scenes were shot in the Tampa area, at Drew and MacDill air fields.

Tracy, Johnson and screenwriter Dalton Trumbo

joined forces again for *30 Seconds Over Tokyo* later that year. Despite the flag-waving patriotism of the scripts, Trumbo was among a group of filmmakers (known collectively as the Hollywood Ten) who were called before the House Committee on Un-American Activities and questioned about ties to the Communist party. When they refused to answer the committee's questions, they were convicted of contempt of Congress.

Trumbo served a brief jail sentence and, like many Hollywood liberals, he was blacklisted for years. During the blacklist, Trumbo had to write under aliases; he even won an Oscar as Robert Rich for writing *The Brave One*. He was finally able to use his real name thirteen years later, when he was credited with writing the scripts for *Exodus* and *Spartacus*.

THE HAPPENING (Columbia - 1967)

Miami
Written by Frank Pierson, James Buchanan, Ronald Austin
Directed by Elliot Silverstein
Starring Anthony Quinn, Faye Dunaway, Robert Walker Jr., George Maharis, Milton Berle

At various points during production, *The Happening* was known as *The Innocent, Mr. Innocent* and *The Young Innocents*. If the producers had been as concerned with the script as they were with the title, the film might have turned out better.

Anthony Quinn and friends

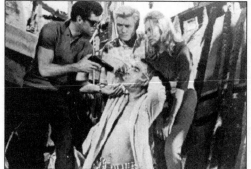

In the comedy, Anthony Quinn stars as a gangster who is kidnapped by a group of beach bums.

As happened to Bette Midler in *Ruthless People*, no one jumps in to pay his ransom, and he ends up helping the kidnappers. The movie is most notable as the film debut of Bascom, Florida, native Faye Dunaway.

HARRY AND SON (Orion - 1984)

Robby Benson and
Paul Newman

Fort Lauderdale
Written by Paul Newman, Ronald Buck
Directed by Paul Newman
Starring Paul Newman, Robby Benson, Ellen Barkin, Joanne Woodward

Paul Newman co-wrote, co-produced, directed and starred in *Harry and Son*. Originally, he wanted to cast Gene Hackman in the lead of this story about a strained relationship between a father and son. In the end, he played father to Robby Benson's son, a relationship that many critics claimed was miscasting. Perhaps the best decision made during production was to finish shooting the movie in time for race-car driver Newman to enter the Trans Am races at Moroso Motor Park in West Palm Beach.

HAVANA (Universal - 1990)

Key West
Written by Judith Rascoe, David Rayfiel
Directed by Sydney Pollack
Starring Robert Redford

Robert Redford and Sydney Pollack collaborated on a string of hits including *Jeremiah Johnson*, *The Way We Were, Three Days of the Condor* and *Out of Africa*. Then came *Havana*.

In the film, Redford plays a gambler who gets caught up in the intrigue of Castro's revolution and falls for Lena Olin. The film was poorly received by audiences and critics, some of whom said it may have signaled the end of the adult romance. Still, those who stayed until the movie's end got to see a great shot of Key West's Smathers' Beach.

(See "On Location")

HEALTH (20th Century-Fox - 1979)

St. Petersburg
Written by Robert Altman, Paul Dooley, Frank Barhydt
Directed by Robert Altman
Starring Lauren Bacall, Glenda Jackson, James Garner, Dick Cavett, Carol Burnett, Alfre Woodard

Like other Robert Altman movies such as *Nashville, A Wedding* and *M*A*S*H, Health* is a satire that features many characters brought together in a single location. The film is set around a health-industry convention, and uses the industry's presidential election to lampoon politics.

Lauren Bacall and James Garner

Health is unlike most films in that it was shot in sequence. The production spent three months filming at the Don Cesar Hotel in St. Petersburg Beach. The film also had the unusual distinction of being denied release by its studio. Altman's previous two films, *Quintet* and *A Perfect Couple*, had performed miserably at the the box office, and Fox feared it had another turkey on its hands.

For his part, Altman claims the snub came because the project had been approved under a different studio regime. Whatever the reason, he personally tried to revive the movie by taking it to film festivals, winning awards in Venice and Montreal. The studio put *Health* in a theater in Los Angeles for a couple of weeks, but then ended distibution altogether and sold the rights to television.

(See "On Location")

THE HEARTBREAK KID (Fox - 1972)

Miami Beach
Written by Neil Simon
Directed by Elaine May
Starring Charles Grodin, Cybill Shepherd, Jeannie Berlin, Eddie Albert

E laine May directed her daughter Jeannie Berlin to an Academy Award nomination in *The Heartbreak Kid*. In the film, newlyweds Berlin and Charles Grodin spend their honeymoon in Miami, where he dumps her and chases after Cybill Shepherd. A University of Miami alumnus, Grodin had appeared in *Catch-22*, which was directed by May's ex-husband and Berlin's father Mike Nichols.

Charles Grodin and
Cybill Shepherd

HELL HARBOR (United Artists - 1930)

Tampa
Written by Clark Silvernail
Directed by Henry King
Starring Lupe Velez, Jean Hersholt

H ell Harbor was the first major studio film shot entirely in Florida. Tampa and surrounding areas double for the Caribbean in this story about descendents of Morgan the Pirate. Talking pictures were still new, and the film tests the boundaries of sound by including atmospheric effects like squeaking shoes. It also offers picturesque views of the Gulf Coast before the invasion of the condominium. Actor Jean Hersholt is best known for his humanitarian activities. He founded the Motion Picture Relief Fund, and the Academy instituted the Jean Hersholt Humanitarian Award, which is given at the annual Oscar ceremonies.

HELLO DOWN THERE (MGM - 1969)

Miami
Written by Frank Telford, John McGreevy
Directed by Jack Arnold
Starring Tony Randall, Janet Leigh, Jim Backus, Roddy McDowall, Richard Dreyfuss

Before *Friday the 13th* and *A Nightmare on Elm Street*, kids used to go see movies like *Hello Down There*. As with their television cousins *The Brady Bunch* and *Batman*, their plots are high on family values, low on serious plotting and littered with dated '60s sets and hip dialogue.

Richard Dreyfuss on bass

In this one, Tony Randall convinces wife Janet Leigh to move their family into in an underwater habitat for a month. The centerpiece of the film was the $100,000 "underwater" set built at the Ivan Tors Studios in North Miami. The underwater scenes were directed by Ricou Browning, who played the monster in *Creature from the Black Lagoon*. Look for Richard Dreyfuss in one of his earliest roles.

A HOLE IN THE HEAD (United Artists - 1959)

Miami Beach
Written by Arnold Shulman
Directed by Frank Capra
Starring Frank Sinatra, Edward G. Robinson, Thelma Ritter

In 1959, Frank Sinatra needed controversy about as much as he needed *A Hole in the Head*, which, coincidentally, is the title of a movie that put him at odds with Miami.

The first film in eight years from legendary director Frank Capra, the comedy stars Sinatra as a widower who (years before Walt Disney World) dreams

Frank Sinatra and
Keenan Wynn

of opening a giant Florida amusement park. Instead, he is saddled with mounting debts and a dying Miami Beach hotel played by The Cardozo Hotel. Desperate for money, he tries to con his business-wise brother Edward G. Robinson, only to be exposed for the fraud that he is.

Much more interesting, however, is the plot that unfolded behind the scenes, where local media cast Sinatra as a spoiled star prone to temper tantrums. When it was announced that the production was leaving Miami earlier than expected, a number of critical stories appeared. Soon, the newspapers were filled with angry responses flying back and forth between Sinatra and the journalists.

The West Flagler Kennel Club upped the ante when it filed suit to destroy footage shot at the club. The producers had gotten permission to film there in exchange for a personal appearance by Sinatra, but the "Chairman of the Board" missed the engagement. The film's publicist claimed that Sinatra was unable to attend due to illness, but his new-found "friends" in the media were eager to point out that he was well enough to attend a cast party the same night.

The night before he left town, Ol' Blue Eyes returned to his hotel room at the Fountainebleu Hotel, only to be greeted by a pair of female deputies who served him papers. (The media did report that he was nice enough to give both deputies autographs.) The Carlyle Hotel rubbed salt into the wound by filing suit claiming that filming at the neighboring Cardozo had become a nuisance. Maybe they just wanted to jump on the publicity bandwagon with the Cardozo and the Fountainebleu.

In the end, the film went on to win an Oscar for the song "High Hopes," but it didn't move any rubber tree plants at the box office. Capra made only one more movie before being "retired" by the industry he had once dominated. Sinatra and Miami worked out their differences, and he came back to film *Tony Rome* and *Lady in Cement*.

(See "On Location")

HONKY TONK FREEWAY (EMI - 1981)

Mount Dora
Written by Edward Clinton
Directed by John Schlesinger
Starring William Devane, Beau Bridges, Teri Garr, Hume Cronyn, Beverly D'Angelo, Jessica Tandy, Howard Hesseman, Geraldine Page

After its release, *Honky Tonk Freeway* won the dubious distinction of having what has been called the worst budget-to-box-office ratio in the history of movies. This may be an exaggeration, but not much of one. The film cost $25,000,000 to make, and raked in a box office total of $500,000—meaning every dollar spent brought back two cents in ticket sales.

As in *Nashville*, the plotting follows numerous characters around a single setting. But, instead of

Tennessee, this one is set in the fictional Florida town of Ticlaw. The people of Ticlaw, led by mayor William Devane, will go to any length to attract tourists by getting an exit off the interstate.

The film is not as bad as its notorious reputation would imply. An award should be given to Mount Dora, which

William Devane and friend

subbed for Ticlaw. The sleepy Central Florida town allowed itself to be painted pink as part of the movie's plot.

(See "On Location")

HOW DO I LOVE THEE? (ABC - 1970)

Miami
Written by Everett Freeman
Directed by Michael Gordon
Starring Jackie Gleason, Maureen O'Hara, Shelley Winters

Jackie Gleason and
Maureen O'Hara

Based on Peter De Vrie's novel *Let Me Count the Ways*, *How Do I Love Thee* is a comedy/drama that never lives up to the talent of its cast members.

Its convoluted plot casts Gleason as an atheist who goes to Lourdes because he thinks his lack of belief has doomed his son to a life of failure. As in *Don't Drink the Water*, the Miami location resulted because star Jackie Gleason liked to stay at home. Unfortunately, so did audiences.

ILLEGALLY YOURS (De Laurentiis - 1988)

St. Augustine
Written by M.A. Stewart, Max Dickens
Directed by Peter Bogdanovich
Starring Rob Lowe, Colleen Camp

Illegally Yours stars Rob Lowe as a juror in a case involving the first girl he ever had a crush on. It is a romantic comedy that, behind the scenes, played out like a Greek tragedy. Act One stars the De Laurentiis Entertainment Group, which financed the film and instantly went bankrupt. In Act Two, director Peter Bogdanovich continues one of the worst career declines in film history.

Finally, Act Three sees the protagonist killed by hubris when the discovery of a home videotape of Rob Lowe having sex with a minor became the scandal of the year. If only the movie had gotten the exposure that the sex video did. It only played in theaters in San Francisco and Texas, where the director was still popular for *The Last Picture Show*.
(See "On Location")

JAWS 2 (Universal - 1978)

Navarre Beach
Written by Carl Gottlieb, Howard Sackler, Dorothy Tristan
Directed by Jeannot Szwarc
Starring Roy Scheider, Lorraine Gary, Murray Hamilton

"Just when you thought it was safe to go back in the water..."
The most famous selling line in movie history.

Until *Star Wars* came along, *Jaws* was the all-time box-office king. Aside from fame and fortune, this meant that there had to be a *Jaws 2*.

Once again, Amity Island is attacked by a giant great white shark. Once again, Roy Scheider manages to overcome his fear of water and kill the sucker. And once again, a whole bunch of people pay to see it.

Back from the original are Lorraine Gary as Scheider's wife and Murray Hamilton as the coverup-minded mayor who still manages to get re-elected. Gary's involvement is no surprise (she even came back for *Jaws: The Revenge*) because her hus-

Lunch time

band is Universal Studios honcho Syd Sheinberg. As for Scheider, he was straightforward about reprising the role of Sheriff Brody. "Jaws is the best damn movie ever made. Jaws 2 is a contractual agreement that I will fulfill as best I can." Method-acting maven Stanislavsky would roll over in his grave.

On the production side of things, the most important task was the construction of the mechanical shark Bruce II (the original Bruce was named after Steven Spielberg's lawyer). Built at a cost of $2,250,000, Bruce II cost as much as a quarter of the budget of the original *Jaws*.

During filming, director John Hancock was replaced by television director Jeannot Szwarc. Other difficulties had the production leave Cape Cod and relocate to Florida. Despite these shakeups, the film was a commercial success and led to two more sequels. Which brings us to...

JAWS 3-D (Universal - 1983)

Orlando
Written by Richard Matheson, Carl Gottlieb
Directed by Joe Alves
Starring Dennis Quaid, Louis Gossett, Jr., Bess Armstrong, Leah Thompson, Simon MacCorkindale

"The third dimension is terror."

No, watching it is terror.

Jaws 3-D is a sequel featuring a 35-foot-long great white shark chasing people around Sea World, a Florida marine park. *Revenge of the Creature* (also filmed in 3-D) is a sequel featuring a water monster chasing people around Marineland, a Florida marine park. Hmm.

Anyway, the movie was directed by Joe Alves, who, as production designer of the fist two movies, helped design the original shark. Dennis Quaid stars as Mike Brody, the now-grown son from the first two movies.

Dan Blasko and Bess Armstrong

Watching *Jaws 3-D* makes a number of questions come to mind: Why doesn't the Brody family just stay out of the water? Do they have "Eat Me" painted on the soles of their feet? How can a shark attack Orlando, which is sixty miles from the ocean? And why is Louis Gossett, Jr. in this movie?

The first three puzzles must be pinned on the writers, but the fourth is the fault of Hollywood's treatment of African-American actors. Following Gossett's Oscar-winning performance in *An Officer and a Gentleman*, *Jaws 3-D* was the only role he was offered. This is a lot scarier than a robot shark attacking a theme park.

(See "On Location")

JOHNNY TIGER (Universal - 1966)

Wekiwa Springs
Written by Paul Crabtree, Thomas Blackburn, Philip Wylie, John Hugh
Directed by Paul Wendkos
Starring Robert Taylor, Chad Everett

There have been no fewer than 37 feature films with titles that begin with the name "Johnny." Undoubtedly, *Johnny Tiger* is one of the worst. This movie about a teacher among the Seminole Indians was produced by longtime Orlando-based independent filmmaker John Hugh. The fact that Universal released it on a double bill with *Munster Go Home* shows the magnitude of their confidence in the project.

LADY IN CEMENT (20th Century-Fox - 1968)

Miami
Written by Marvin H. Albert, Jack Guss
Directed by Gordon Douglas
Starring Frank Sinatra, Raquel Welch, Richard Conte, Lainie Kazan

FrankSinatra and Raquel Welch

While diving for treasure, private eye Frank Sinatra discovers a female corpse on the ocean floor. So begins *Lady in Cement*, the sequel to the previous year's *Tony Rome*. Hoping that the hard-boiled detective would catch on with audiences, the sequel was already being planned while the original was still in production.

While filming *A Hole in the Head*, Sinatra became the focus of press attacks and a lawsuit when he failed to show up for a personal appearance at a racetrack. Maybe he should have given some advice to co-star Raquel Welch. This time around, she drew newspaper criticism for failing to show at the position drawing for the Florida Derby. It turns out that filming had run late and her hair wasn't ready.

The shooting schedule for *Lady in Cement* fit well into Sinatra's entertainment schedule at the Fountainebleu, where he put on a one-man show during production. Because he was moonlighting, filming could begin no earlier than 10 a.m.

A LADY WITHOUT PASSPORT (MGM - 1950)

The Everglades
Written by Howard Dimsdale
Directed by Joseph H. Lewis
Starring Hedy Lamarr, John Hodiak

Florida hasn't been very kind to Hedy Lamarr. Fresh from her success in *Samson and Delilah*, she came to the Sunshine State to star in *A Lady Without Passport*, a drama about efforts to stop illegal aliens coming into the country from the Caribbean.

Unfortunately, the studio decided to cut corners on the film, and didn't give her big-name stars to back her up. *Lady* wound up being a B picture. Lamarr's treatment was no better forty years later: In 1991, she was arrested for shoplifting at an Orlando-area drugstore (the charge was later dropped) and nobody recognized her.

Hedy Lamarr and
John Hodiak

LENNY (United Artists - 1974)

Miami
Written by Julian Barry
Directed by Bob Fosse
Starring Dustin Hoffman, Valerie Perrine, Gary Morton

"Allegedly, Lenny is to be a prestigious film."
A skeptical Miami journalist during preproduction. (The film went on to recieve six Academy Award nominations, including one for Best Picture.)

Based on Julian Barry's Broadway play, *Lenny* uses flashbacks, interviews and a documentary style to tell the story of Lenny Bruce. Perhaps more than any other comedian, Bruce divided his audiences, who found him either extremely funny or extremely offensive. Always on the cutting edge of humor, his routines sometimes landed him in jail.

Lenny allows present-day audiences to judge the humor for themselves. Dustin Hoffman was meticulous in his research, and does many of Bruce's actual routines. Likewise, director Bob Fosse's use of black-and-white film and cramped locations recreates the dark intimacy of the nightclubs where Bruce performed.

Dustin Hoffman and
Valerie Perrine

Even after his death, Bruce divided audiences. While some Miamians heralded the coming film, others condemned it as pornography. The filmmakers were even kept from filming trial scenes inside the Dade County Courthouse, after a judge read a copy of the script. Despite protestations from government officials in Tallahassee, the judge held his ground, offering the hard-to-swallow excuse that it would put the court in an awkward position should the film be banned in theaters.

LET IT RIDE (Paramount - 1989)

Hialeah
Written by Nancy Dowd
Directed by Joe Pytka
Starring Richard Dreyfuss, Teri Garr, David Johansen

"He drinks. He smokes. He gambles. He curses. He thinks about committing adultery. You'll love him."

Wishful thinking from the Paramount publicity department.

S mall movies are supposed to be the antidote to the type of big-budget commercial films that open every weekend during the summer. With no special effects, car chases or high-concept plotting, they win over audiences by presenting endearing characters and offbeat storylines.

David Johansen and
Richard Dreyfuss

The Richard Dreyfuss movie *Tin Men* is a perfect example of a successful small movie. Unfortunately, *Tin Men* was made in Baltimore. In Florida, Richard Dreyfuss starred in the movie *Let It Ride*, which is a perfect example of why there are more big-budget movies than small movies.

Dreyfuss plays a Miami cabbie who promises wife Teri Garr that he'll quit gambling, only to go on an incredible winning streak at the racetrack. The problem with small movies is that if the character doesn't endear himself to you, there's not much else in the movie to keep your interest. Music fans will be happy to see David Johansen (aka Buster Poindexter) turn in a good job as Dreyfuss's best friend. Director Joe Pytka also directed the Pepsi commercial during which Michael Jackson's hair caught on fire.

LETHAL WEAPON 3 (Warner Brothers - 1992)

Orlando
Written by Jeffrey Boam
Directed by Richard Donner
Starring Mel Gibson, Danny Glover

Mel Gibson and Danny Glover brought the house down—literally—for the opening of *Lethal Weapon 3*. The movie picks up with the police partners during the final days before Glover's

retirement from the force. The International Control Systems building that explodes at the beginning of the movie was Orlando's City Hall for thirty-three years.

The scene was written into the script when the producers learned that the former city hall was to be imploded. Appropriately, the head of the bomb squad was played by Orlando mayor Bill Frederick, whose real-life office had just been destroyed.

City Hall takes a
Lethal fall

LICENCE TO KILL (MGM/UA - 1989)

Key West
Written by Richard Maibaum, Michael Wilson
Directed by John Glen
Starring Timothy Dalton

"A farewell to arms."
James Bond's witty reference as he disarms an opponent at Key West's Hemingway House.

Although a number of James Bond films were shot in Florida, none spent as much time in the state as *Licence to Kill*. Too bad it's one of the least successful in the Bond series. Timothy Dalton, as Agent 007, goes on a vendetta against bad guy Robert Davi to avenge a brutal attack on a friend. This leads the powers that be to revoke his license to kill. The film

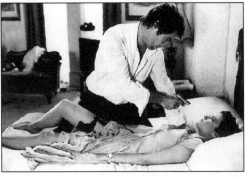

was originally to be titled *Licence Revoked*, but research showed that too many people didn't know the meaning of the word "revoked." The producers did decide to use the British spelling of the word "license," which caused massive confusion on theater marquees.

Timothy Dalton and
Carey Lowell

In the movie, Florida Governor Bob Martinez plays an airline ticket customer. He initially suggested that he appear in the movie, and the producers said no, thank you. Still, he visited the set during production and politely suggested again that he be cast in the film. This time, the producers relented. Martinez later used a similar technique to get himself cast as the nation's drug czar.

(See "On Location")

MAKING MR. RIGHT (Orion - 1987)

Miami
Writing by Floyd Byars, Laurie Frank
Directed by Susan Seidelman
Starring John Malkovich, Ann Magnuson, Laurie Metcalf

Once, while doing a play with Chicago's famed Steppenwolf Theater, John Malkovich painted on a sideburn in the shape of Florida and put a star where Tallahassee would be. No word on whether this was part of a subliminal campaign by the Florida tourism board, but the state was certainly happy when he came to Miami to play dual roles in *Making Mr. Right*.

Malkovich stars as both a scientist and the robot

he creates in this movie. Performance artist Ann Magnuson (who later gained fame on the television series *Anything But Love*) is the publicist who falls in love with the robot at the same time she is creating his public image.

Making Mr. Right is exactly the type of movie that separated Orion from other studios. It has an unusual but talented cast and the greatest of Hollywood rarities—a woman director. Susan Seidelman, who also directed *Desperately Seeking Susan* for the studio, had nothing but praise for Orion during production. "The way Orion operates is perfect. They were on the set the first week and then they were gone." Unfortunately, while such freedom and risk-taking made for wonderful, award-winning movies, it also drove the studio into bankruptcy.

MARRIED TO THE MOB (Orion - 1988)

Miami
Written by Barry Strugatz, Mark R. Burns
Directed by Jonathan Demme
Starring Michelle Pfeiffer, Dean Stockwell

Another example of Orion's loopy sensibilities, *Married to the Mob* was directed by Jonathan Demme, whose career didn't get the credit it deserved until he made *The Silence of the Lambs.* In

Dean Stockwell and Michelle Pfeiffer

Mob, Michelle Pfeiffer stars as a woman who does her best to break free of Mafia connections after her hit man husband is "rubbed out." Dean Stockwell won rave reviews and an Oscar nomination for his portrayal of the Mafia boss Tony "The Tiger" Russo. Most of the film takes place in New York, but

the final scenes concern a Florida mob convention reminiscent of the one in *Some Like It Hot*.
(See "On Location")

THE MEAN SEASON (Orion - 1985)

Miami
Written by Leon Piedmont
Directed by Philip Borsos
Starring Kurt Russell, Mariel Hemingway, Richard Jordan, Andy Garcia

"I don't want to see my name in the paper next to photos of dead bodies anymore."
Kurt Russell proving that journalists have some standards.

*A*bsence of Malice and *The Mean Season* comprise the "Miami reporter crosses the line and becomes the story" subgenre of filmmaking. Based on John Katzenbach's novel *In the Heat of the Summer*, the movie uses the deadly tropical storm season as a backdrop.

In the film, serial killer Richard Jordan contacts journalist Kurt Russell and gives him exclusive stories about his killing spree. But Jordan gets jealous when Russell's involvement makes him a celebrity, taking attention away from the killer.
(See "On Location")

MIAMI BLUES (Orion - 1990)

Miami
Written and Directed by George Armitage
Starring Alec Baldwin, Fred Ward, Jennifer Jason Leigh

*Y*ou know that *Miami Blues* is an unusual movie right from the start, when Alec Baldwin breaks the finger of a Hare Krishna at the Miami

International Airport and the Krishna goes into shock and dies. (The film's finger fixation continues later when Baldwin has a couple sliced off.)

In the film, which was produced by Jonathan Demme, Baldwin plays a psychopathic killer who longs to lead an average, middle-class lifestyle. He even sets up house with prostitute Jennifer Jason Leigh, who has similar longings. But Baldwin can't shake that urge to kill and ultimately does battle with homicide cop Fred Ward. The violence and offbeat nature kept audiences away, but the film already has a certain cult following. There are also rumors that it has cut down on solicitors at the Miami airport.

MIDNIGHT COWBOY (United Artists - 1969)

Miami
Written by Waldo Salt
Directed by John Schlesinger
Starring Jon Voight, Dustin Hoffman

"Hey, Ratso, wake up. We're here. We're in Miami."
Jon Voight talking to a dead Dustin Hoffman at the end of *Midnight Cowboy.*

Because of changes in the rating system, *Midnight Cowboy* is assured of its place as the only X-rated film to win the Oscar for Best Picture. This dark story of street hustler Jon Voight and his tubercular

Jon Voight and
Dustin Hoffman

best friend Dustin Hoffman puts a spin on the standard symbolism of Florida's paradise. Throughout the movie, the drifters talk of escaping the New York winter for the Sunshine State. But Miami is paradise unfulfilled, with Hoffman dying on the bus just as they arrive.

MR. PEABODY AND THE MERMAID (Universal - 1948)

Weeki Wachee
Written by Nunnally Johnson
Directed by Irving Pichel
Starring William Powell, Ann Blyth

Ann Blyth and William Powell

Weeki Wachee is known for its mermaids, who perform and even drink RC Cola underwater. In 1948, the attraction provided some locations for the Universal picture *Mr. Peabody and the Mermaid*. In the movie, fifty-year-old William Powell takes a vacation to combat a mid-life crisis. While out fishing, he hooks mermaid Ann Blyth. They fall in love, but interspecies relationships can be difficult—witness Tom Hanks and Darryl Hannah in SPLASH.

MY GIRL (Columbia - 1991)

Sanford
Written by Laurice Elehwany
Directed by Howard Zieff
Starring Dan Aykroyd, Jamie Lee Curtis, Macaulay Culkin, Anna Chlumsky

A funny thing happened right before cameras started rolling on *My Girl*. *Home Alone*, featuring *My Girl* co-star Macaulay Culkin, started breaking box-office records and went on to become the highest-grossing comedy in film history. Contracts had to be renogotiated, and Culkin wound up with a million-dollar deal. As if that weren't enough, Culkin and newcomer Anna Chlumsky earned some spending cash by fining adults who swore on the set. (Going rates were $5 for the "s-word" and $10 for the "f-word.")

A pleasant change, *My Girl* is a coming-of-age movie about a girl rather than a boy. Chlumsky plays the daughter of widowed mortician Dan Aykroyd. We watch her neuroses and heartbreaks through her friendship with Culkin and her father's budding relationship with beautician Jamie Lee Curtis.

Originally scheduled to film at Universal Studios, the movie wound up shooting interiors in an abandoned studio in southwest Orlando. The highlight of production was the Jamie Lee Curtis Florida Invitational Ping-Pong Tournament, in which the crew competed spiritedly, to say the least. Meanwhile, Culkin and Chlumsky had typical kid-type activities such as a spelling bee, which Chlumsky won.

Macaulay Culkin and
Anna Chlumsky

Determined to take advantage of Culkin's popularity, Columbia's ad campaign hardly mentioned grownups Aykroyd and Curtis. Instead, it centered on the kids, using the slogan "Mac is Back."

The film created a controversy when it was released. Some critics and parents were outraged that Culkin's character dies in a film aimed at children. Interestingly, not many of these critics and parents had been outraged a year earlier when, in *Home Alone*, Culkin shot Daniel Stern with a BB gun, set Joe Pesci's hair on fire and invented all sorts of violent acts. It seems that violence is okay, but God forbid that children should learn about mortality.

(See: "On Location")

NEPTUNE'S DAUGHTER (MGM - 1949)

Weeki Wachee
Written by Dorothy Kingsley
Directed by Edward Buzzell
Starring Esther Williams, Red Skelton, Keenan Wynn, Ricardo Montalban, Xavier Cugat

It's appropriate that "Hollywood's Mermaid" would make a movie at Florida's mermaid attraction: Weeki Wachee. The loose plotting of *Neptune's Daughter* features Esther Williams and Keenan Wynn as partners in a bathing-suit company. Of course, this provides Williams with many opportunities to get wet and sing. The film is most memorable for its Oscar-winning song "Baby It's Cold Outside."

Keenan Wynn and Esther Williams

Realism being a minor component of such films, one of the movie's highlights occurs when Williams is raised from the water wearing a head-dress of lit sparklers. If you watch on videotape, you can reverse the action and see that she is actually being lowered into the water, which extinguishes all of her sparklers.

(See "On Location")

A NIGHT IN HEAVEN (20th Century-Fox - 1984)

Titusville
Written by Joan Tewkesbury
Directed by John Avildsen
Starring Christopher Atkins, Leslie Ann Warren

Florida hasn't been too kind to the creatures from the *Blue Lagoon*. After co-starring together, Brooke Shields and Christopher Atkins have

Chris Atkins and
Leslie Ann Warren

both struck dirt, not gold, in the Sunshine State. Shields was done in by *Brenda Starr* and Atkins by *A Night in Heaven*.

Atkins plays a college student who leads a double life as a male stripper. He seduces his professor, played by Leslie Ann Warren. Perhaps the critical opinion of the film was best summed up by *People* magazine, which said, "No title would be idiotic enough to reflect the mindlessness of this film." Other notables involved in the production are director John Avildsen (who actually won an Oscar once for directing *Rocky*) and Deney Terrio, who was the longtime host of *Dance Fever*.

NIGHT MOVES (Warner Brothers - 1975)

Sanibel Island
Written by Alan Sharp
Directed by Arthur Penn
Starring Gene Hackman, Melanie Griffith, Susan Clark, James Woods, Jennifer Warren

"Maybe he would find the girl...maybe he would find himself."
Good selling line; too bad he couldn't find an audience.

Gene Hackman, Melanie
Griffith and Jennifer Warren

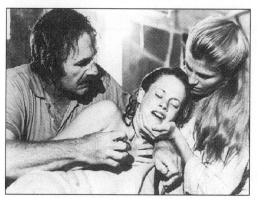

Gene Hackman plays a disillusioned private eye in *Night Moves*. In the film, Hackman comes to Florida in search of missing heiress Melanie Griffith.

The film provided the screen debut for Griffith and reunited Hackman with Arthur Penn, who had directed the actor to an Oscar nomination in *Bonnie and Clyde* eight years earlier.

Although set in the Keys, the movie's primary Florida location was Sanibel Island, on the southwest coast.

92 IN THE SHADE (United Artists - 1975)

Key West
Written and directed by Thomas McGuane
Starring Peter Fonda, Warren Oates, Margo Kidder, Harry Dean Stanton, Elizabeth Ashley

Unhappy with the way that his novels *The Sporting Club* and *Rancho Deluxe* had been translated into movies, Thomas McGuane decided to write and direct his own film version of *92 In the Shade*. The plot surrounds a cutthroat vendetta between Peter Fonda and Warren Oates, a pair of Key West fishing guides.

Although it was not a commercial success, the film has something of a cult reputation. It also spawned a romance between McGuane and actress Elizabeth Ashley. Six years later, a different version of the film was released with a less tragic ending, in the hopes of attracting a bigger audience. It didn't.

THE NORSEMAN (American International - 1978)

Tampa
Written and Directed by Charles Pierce
Starring Lee Majors, Cornel Wilde, Mel Ferrer

The *Norseman* was produced by Fawcett-Majors Productions, back when Farah and the Six Million Dollar Man were still together. In the movie, Majors plays Thorvald, who leads a group of wool-clad, horn-hatted, 11th-century vikings on an expedition to North America. Rather than landing in Nova Scotia or New England, however, they wind up trampling through West Florida and the Everglades. That pretty much says it all.

ON AN ISLAND WITH YOU (MGM - 1948)

Key Biscayne
Written by Dorothy Kingsley, Dorothy Cooper, Charles Martin, Hans Wilhelm
Directed by Richard Thorpe
Starring Esther Williams, Peter Lawford, Jimmy Durante, Ricardo Montalban, Cyd Charrisse

"In California, we got trees. In California, we got sand. In California, we got oceans. But, here, we also got bugs."
Esther Williams on the joys of filming in Florida.

Ricardo Montalban and
Esther Williams

On an Island With You was Esther Williams's first trip to Florida, where the bugs were so bad that she had to mix insect repellent into her pancake makeup. Key Biscayne doubles for Hawaii, where Williams is a movie star on location. She gets kidnapped by smitten Navy pilot Peter Lawford, who takes her to a deserted island so she can perform personalized musical numbers for him.

OPERATION PETTICOAT (Universal - 1959)

Key West
Written by Stanley Shapiro, Maurice Richlin
Directed by Blake Edwards
Starring Cary Grant, Tony Curtis, Joan O'Brien, Dina Merrill

Before Cary Grant agreed to star in the film, *Operation Petticoat* was scheduled to be a black-and-white movie with a budget of only a million dollars. However, a friend of the producer slipped Grant a copy of the script. Once he agreed to play the lead, the budget tripled, and the black and white was shelved for color.

Tony Curtis and friends

Grant stars as the commander of the USS *Sea Tiger*, a submarine that must face the humilation of carrying a load of nurses and refugee Filipino children, and the ultimate embarrassment of being painted pink.

Filmed in Key West aboard the submarine USS *Balboa*, the production teamed Tony Curtis with his idol Grant.

The year before, Curtis had perfectly mimicked Grant while seducing Marilyn Monroe in *Some Like It Hot*. He had refined the accent while serving at sea in World War II. The ship he was on had a limited number of movies, one of which was *Gunga Din*. After countless viewings, the crew would turn off the sound and recite the lines by rote. Curtis was always cast in Grant's role.

Box office for the comedy was huge, and at the time the film was Universal's all-time biggest money earner. Especially pleased was Grant, whose contract was built around box-office percentages. He netted three million dollars on the film, which up till then was a record amount paid to a single actor.

Grant got Dina Merrill, a cousin of his former wife Barbara Hutton, cast in the role of Nurse Duran. Two other cast members went on to become television stars: Nurse Colfax was played by Marion Ross, who later went on to star in *Happy Days*; seaman Hunkle was played by Gavin McLeod, who later captained *The Love Boat*.

OSCAR (Touchstone - 1991)

Orlando
Written by Michael Barrie, Jim Mulholland
Directed by John Landis
Starring Sylvester Stallone

When action star Arnold Schwarzenegger said he was going to make comedies, everybody laughed. Then he laughed all the way to the bank with *Twins* and *Kindergarten Cop*, and Sylvester Stallone started looking for comedy scripts. He decided on *Oscar*, a screwball comedy about Snaps

Sly Stallone and John Landis

Provolone, a gangster who wants to get into legitimate business.

The entire story takes place on a single day in Provolone's neighborhood. Production began on the backlot of Universal Studios Hollywood. But, with filming halfway done, a fire destroyed much of the Universal backlot, including the sets for *Oscar*. Filming had to be postponed, then relocated to Universal Studios Florida, where the neighborhood set was meticulously reconstructed.

John Landis was picked to direct the film based on his successful string of comedies, including

Animal House, The Blues Brothers, Trading Places, The Three Amigos and *Coming to America*. However, all of these films starred the best and brightest of the television show *Saturday Night Live*. Paired with conventional actors, Landis has delivered such forgettable fare as *Into the Night, The Twilight Zone* and the *Thriller* video.

Under normal circumstances, the set would have become a featured attraction on the Universal Studios Florida tour. But *Oscar* is a Disney movie, and Disney didn't want to contribute a set to the chief competition to its Disney/MGM Studios. After a few weeks of production, everything that was meticulously reconstructed was swiftly deconstructed. Universal got the last laugh, though, when audiences stayed away from the picture in droves.

(See "On Location")

PAPER LION (United Artists - 1968)

Boca Raton
Written by Lawrence Roman
Directed by Alex March
Starring Alan Alda, Lauren Hutton, Alex Karras

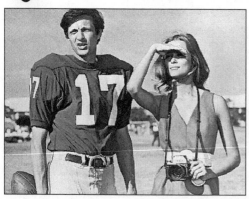

Alan Alda and Lauren Hutton

Paper Lion is the type of movie that studio publicity departments hate. Other than the best-selling book that it was based on, the film had almost no marketable elements when it was released. First of all, sports movies are traditionally box-office poison. Secondly, director Alex March was fired during production and his duties taken over by the film's producer. More importantly, it featured a cast consisting of a relatively unknown actor, a fashion model in her film debut and a number of celebrated non-acting athletes portraying themselves.

Alan Alda, in only his second movie, plays writer George Plimpton, who was known as "the amateur professional" because of his many head-to-head contests with professional athletes. For various books and articles, Plimpton had pitched against a lineup of baseball all-stars, fought a few rounds against a champion boxer and tried out for quarterback of the Detroit Lions.

In real life, Alda's mother had made him quit football in high school because she was fearful that it might hurt his braces. Here, he had to go up against real NFL players, who took advantage of every opportunity to remind him that he was an actor and they were athletes. During production, Alex Karras expressed an interest in pursuing an acting career after retiring from football. While it may have seemed unlikely at the time, he did go on to star in his own successful television series, *Webster*.

PARENTHOOD (Universal - 1989)

Orlando
Written by Lowell Ganz, Babaloo Mandel
Directed by Ron Howard
Starring Steve Martin, Mary Steenburgen, Dianne Wiest, Jason Robards, Rick Moranis, Keanu Reeves, Martha Plimpton, Tom Hulce

"It could happen to you."

Effective selling line.

Parenthood provided Orlando with its breakthrough into big-budget feature films. Director Ron Howard and an all-star cast filmed the entire movie in Central Florida, using multiple locations. The film christened the sound stages at

Steve Martin

Universal Studios Florida. (For features, anyway; the low-budget film *The Spring* actually used the studio first.)

Set in St. Louis, the film concerns the ups and downs of parenting as experienced by four generations of the same family. As a team, director Howard and screenwriters Ganz and Mandel do an excellent job of weaving the storylines of a movie that features seventeen principal cast members. Ganz and Mandel first met Howard as writers on the sitcom *Happy Days*. They went on to write his films *Night Shift*, *Splash* and *Gung Ho*.

For her work in *Parenthood*, Dianne Wiest was nominated for an Oscar for Best Supporting Actress.

(See "On Location")

PASSENGER 57 (Warner Brothers - 1992)

Orlando
Written by David Loughery
Directed by Kevin Hooks
Starring Wesley Snipes

When she retired, famed movie critic Pauline Kael complained about the present state of filmmaking. She went on to say that, in an industry of mediocrity, one of the few positives was Wesley Snipes, who had starred in such films as *New Jack City* and *Jungle Fever*. Snipes, who went to Jones High School in Orlando, had climbed from supporting roles to become one of Hollywood's few African-American leading men.

Passenger 57 allowed him an opportunity to return to his hometown with all the trappings of celebrity. As a treat for his alma mater, Snipes cast more than twenty Jones High School honor students in the carnival chase scene. The production spent eleven weeks in Orlando, Sanford and at the Disney/MGM Studios. Snipes plays a security expert battling terrorist Bruce Payne in an airplane 30,000 feet up. He has to keep Payne from hijacking the plane before it arrives in Los Angeles, where Payne is due to stand trial. This is the second feature film directed by Kevin Hooks, one of several successful directors to come from the cast of the television show *The White Shadow*.

POLICE ACADEMY 5: ASSIGNMENT MIAMI BEACH
(Warner Brothers - 1988)

Miami
Written by Stephen J. Curwick
Directed by Alan Myerson
Starring Bubba Smith, Matt McCoy, Michael Winslow, Janet Jones

Just when you thought you had figured out the *Police Academy* formula, they throw you a curve ball and set the movie in Miami. For all you *Academy* aficionados—and you must be out there or else they wouldn't keep making them—this is the longest of the five sequels, and the first to try to make it without Steve Guttenberg leading the way. It also put a few million dollars into the South Florida economy, provided jobs for hundreds of people and let Michael Winslow make those funny noises. It's still inexcusable.

POPI (United Artists - 1969)

Miami
Written by Tina Pine, Les Pine
Directed by Arthur Hiller
Starring Alan Arkin, Rita Moreno

In *Popi*, Alan Arkin plays a poor widower living in New York's Spanish Harlem. Worried that he cannot provide for his two sons, he takes them to Miami and puts them on a raft, hoping that they will be discovered and adopted by a wealthy family mistaking them for Cuban refugees.

During production, the two boys playing the sons didn't want to strip bare for the refugee scenes. At wits' end to overcome their modesty, director Arthur Hiller took off his own clothes. His willingness convinced the boys, and they followed suit.

PORKY'S (20th Century-Fox - 1982)

Fort Lauderdale
Written and Directed by Bob Clark
Starring Kim Cattral, Alex Karras

Financed in Canada and filmed in Florida, *Porky's* is crude, mindless and somehow managed to change the film world. The low-budget comedy, which follows the sexual exploits of a group of teenagers at Angel Beach High, turned gross into grosses to become one of the most profitable movies in history. Its $100-million box office launched a fleet of copycat teen/sex movies, along with two sequels also shot in Fort Lauderdale.

Examining the *Porky's* trilogy, a philosophical line can be drawn separating the first pair of films, directed by series creator Bob Clark, from the third, which was directed by James Komack.

The theme of civil rights lies at the core of both films directed by Clark, who based the original on his teenage experiences in Florida. In *Porky's* the students fight anti-Semitism, and in *Porky's II: The Next Day* they battle the racism of the Ku Klux Klan and a censorship-minded preacher. Together, the films explore freedom of religion and separation of church and state.

Angel Beach co-eds

In *Porky's Revenge*, however, Komack redefines the Porky's oeuvre by supplanting civil rights with a theme of corruption: Gamblers attempt to fix the high-school basketball state championship game. Furthermore, Porky's roadhouse is replaced by a riverboat casino/brothel, which symbolizes the destructive nature of capitalism.

These lofty themes account for about 2 percent of the films' content. The other 98 percent pretty much deals with a group of hormone-crazed teenage boys who spy on, and try to sleep with, large-breasted women.

PROBLEM CHILD 2 (Universal - 1981)

Orlando
Written by Scott Alexander, Larry Karaszewski
Directed by Brian Levant
Starring John Ritter

*P*roblem Child was a surprise box-office hit for Universal. *Problem Child 2* wasn't. The film did allow director Brian Levant to return to Universal Studios Florida, where he had previously been top dog on *The New Leave It to Beaver* television series. Any triumphant feelings Levant had upon moving from television to feature films must have been negated by the movie's poor public reception.

PT-109 (Warner Brothers - 1963)

Little Palm Island
Written by Richard L. Breen
Directed by Leslie H. Martinson
Starring Cliff Robertson, James Gregory, Robert Blake

It's difficult to make a movie about a living person. This is especially true if that person happens to be the President of the United States. This is the problem that faced the producers of *PT-109*, which tells of the wartime heroics displayed by naval officer John F. Kennedy. Extra precautions were taken to please the administration. Studio chief Jack Warner even took it upon himself to supervise production personally.

Cliff Robertson

The principal difficulty was casting someone to play the lead. Many rumors have circulated about the selection process. One has the FBI running security checks on potential leads to ensure that they were proper to play the President. Another has Warren Beatty rejecting the part when he learns that the White House has final approval. Whatever the process, the role eventually fell to Cliff Robertson, whom JFK himself is said to have personally selected.

There was equal difficulty deciding on a director. Originally slated for Raoul Walsh, the film opened with Lewis Milestone behind the camera. During production, Milestone was fired and replaced by Leslie Martinson. A few months after the film's release, President

Kennedy was assasinated, and Warner Brothers withdrew the film from circulation for several years.

The palm trees on Little Palm Island (aka Munson Island) led to its being cast as the South Pacific setting for the movie. Location shooting proved beneficial for the island when Kennedy decided to visit during production. In anticipation of the President's visit, the island was outfitted with "luxuries" such as electricity, running water and telephone lines.

(See "On Location")

QUICK CHANGE (Warner Brothers - 1991)

Orlando
Written by Howard Franklin
Directed by Bill Murray, Howard Franklin
Starring Bill Murray, Geena Davis, Randy Quaid, Jason Robards

In *Quick Change*, Bill Murray robs a bank in New York, then spends the rest of the movie trying to make it to the airport for his getaway. The final scenes on the airplane were filmed on the Delta L-1011 mockup at the Disney/MGM Studios.

REVENGE OF THE CREATURE (Universal - 1955)

Marineland, Silver Springs
Directed by Jack Arnold
Starring John Agar, Lori Nelson, John Bromfield, Ricou Browning, Clint Eastwood

This sequel to *Creature from the Black Lagoon* has the hapless Creature removed from the Amazon and imprisoned in a tank at Marineland. He breaks free from the tank and terrorizes the park. The film is most notable for the "young lab technician with no name." He is Clint Eastwood, making his screen debut.

THE ROSE TATTOO (Paramount - 1955)

Key West
Written by Tennessee Williams, Hal Kanter
Directed by Daniel Mann
Starring Anna Magnani, Burt Lancaster

The Rose Tattoo is the screen adaptation of Tennessee Williams's play. Anna Magnani stars as a Sicilian-born dressmaker who is torn between her devotion to her dead husband and her attraction to Burt Lancaster.

When he wrote the play, Williams created the

role for the Italian actress, only to have her turn down an offer to play the part on Broadway because she was unsure of her English skills. Five years later, her English was good enough for her to make this film her American screen debut. It proved a wise decision, as she won the Best Actress Oscar for her performance.

Anna Magnani and
Burt Lancaster

RUDE AWAKENING (Orion - 1989)

Wekiwa Springs
Written by Neil Levy, Richard LaGravenese
Directed by Aaron Russo, David Greenwalt
Starring Eric Roberts, Cheech Marin

There was a time when Julia Roberts was known as the sister of Eric Roberts. But despite his two Oscar nominations, Eric is now best known as the brother of Julia. In *Rude Awakening*, he and Cheech Marin are hippies who hide out from the government for twenty years in a Central American jungle. When they return to the States, they find their '60s mentality at odds with the go-go days of the Reagan Revolution. Wekiwa Springs, north of Orlando, is the jungle.

RUNNING SCARED (MGM-UA - 1986)

Key West
Written by Gary Devore, Jimmy Huston
Directed by Peter Hyams
Starring Billy Crystal, Gregory Hines

In the middle of *Running Scared*, Chicago policemen Billy Crystal and Gregory Hines go on vacation to Key West, where they find that life is fun, fishing is good and people actually stand out on

Billy Crystal

Mallory Square to watch the sunset. So happy are they, that they decide to buy a bar and retire here. But first, they have to go finish catching all of the bad guys, so they return to a dreary-looking Chicago. Rarely does a location get such a positive portrayal in a film. The entire Key West sequence might as well have been a paid commercial. (In fact, much of it was used in Michael McDonald's music video for "Sweet Freedom," which was on the film's soundtrack.)

(See "On Location")

SCARFACE (Universal - 1983)

Miami
Written by Oliver Stone
Directed by Brian De Palma
Starring Al Pacino, Steven Bauer, Michelle Pfeiffer, Mary Elizabeth Mastrantonio, Robert Loggia

It has been said that Fidel Castro's favorite movie is *The Godfather*, because he feels the immigrant's rise into organized crime shows how the "American Dream" really works. It would be interesting to hear his reaction to *Scarface*. Few films

Al Pacino and Steven Bauer

carry reputations as notorious as this remake of the 1932 classic. It begins with Castro's wholesale deportation of Cubans to the United States. One of the refugees is Tony Montana, who is played by *The Godfather*'s Al Pacino.

In place of the original's Prohibition-era Chicago, this *Scarface* is set in the drug underworld of Miami. Pacino climbs the ranks to cocaine kingpin, fighting trafficker Robert Loggia and stealing his mistress Michelle Pfeiffer, in her first dramatic role. Like the original Scarface, he has an overprotective and incestuous interest in his sister, played by then unknown Mary Elizabeth Mastrantonio.

The film's notorious reputation began during production. Leery of its portrayal of Cuban Americans, Miami civic leaders and journalists led a charge that actually drove the production out of Florida. Its notoriety was compounded when the MPAA ratings board originally gave the film an X rating, which virtually would have kept it out of theaters. The filmmakers appealed and the board changed the rating to an R, but the critics were waiting. Reviews attacked the film for its gratuitous and excessive violence and foul language. The *Guinness Book of World Records* points out that the so-called "f-word" is spoken in the film an average of once every 29 seconds.

Most of the critical anger was vented at director Brian De Palma and screenwriter Oliver Stone. De Palma's career has been filled with violent homage to other filmmakers, and the always controversial Stone was just about to hit it big as the director of *Salvador* and *Platoon*. Many critics found it insulting that the film was dedicated to Howard Hawks and Ben Hecht, the director and writer responsible for the original.

SEMI-TOUGH (United Artists - 1977)

Miami
Written by Walter Bernstein
Directed by Michael Ritchie
Starring Burt Reynolds, Kris Kristofferson, Jill Clayburgh, Bert Convy, Robert Preston, Roger E. Mosley

"Where were you when I made *The Longest Yard*?"
Burt Reynolds to the Miami film commissioner on the set of *Semi-Tough*.

Burt Reynolds and
Kris Kristofferson

Burt Reynolds likes to play football in his home state. In college, he played for the Florida State Seminoles. He was the natural choice for lead in the prison football movie *The Longest Yard*. But when he came back to film it here, he was greeted with excessive red tape, which drove the production up to Georgia.

Three years later, Reynolds gave Florida another chance with *Semi-Tough*. This time the state was ready. Although Dan Jenkins' book is set in New York, United Artists was convinced to switch the setting to Florida, in great part by Miami Dolphins owner Joe Robbie. Robbie then turned around and rented the Orange Bowl to the studio for $40,000 a day.

It wasn't hard to get extras—fans filled the stands to watch Reynolds and Kris Kristofferson. The studio even convinced many of them to wear ski caps and coats in 80-degree heat, in order to simulate a game in Denver. The hard part was getting a group of women to stop chanting "We want Kris" instead of "We want a touchdown."

As well as lampooning professional football, the movie skewers self-help movements like EST and pyramid power. It also invents a nose-massage therapy called "pelfing" and "Movagenics," a therapy that makes patients crawl like a baby. A television series based on the movie, starring David Hasselhoff, debuted in 1980 and lasted only three weeks before being cancelled.

SEMINOLE (Universal - 1953)

The Everglades
Written by Charles K. Peck, Jr.
Directed by Budd Boetticher
Starring Rock Hudson, Barbara Hale, Anthony Quinn

Anthony Quinn plays the famous Indian Chief Osceola in *Seminole*, which stars Rock Hudson as a West Point graduate assigned to a fort in his home state of Florida. Lee Marvin plays a soldier in one of his first roles. As in many Hollywood treatments of Native Americans, the Seminoles aren't well-depicted in this action film. In contrast to its battle heroics in the film, the Army captured the real Osceola under a phony flag of truce.

SLATTERY'S HURRICANE (Fox - 1949)

Miami
Written by Herman Wouk, Richard Murphy
Directed by Andre de Toth
Starring Richard Widmark, Linda Darnell, Veronica Lake

Slattery's Hurricane is a melodrama about the weather bureau's hurricane-hunter pilots. It stars Miami native Veronica Lake, who was married to director

Veronica Lake and friends

Andre de Toth. One of the biggest actresses of the '40s, Lake was famous for her over-the-eye peekaboo hairstyle. During World War II, government officials requested that she cut her hair, because working women who emulated the style were being injured when their hair got caught in machinery.

Tragically, the style change marked the downfall of Lake's career, and *Slattery* proved to be her last major role. Soon after, she and de Toth declared bankruptcy and she disappeared from public life. Lake was later discovered to be working as a New York barmaid. Her final film was the low-budget horror film *Flesh Feast*, which was also produced in South Florida.

SMOKEY AND THE BANDIT II (Universal - 1980)

Jupiter, The Burt Reynolds Ranch
Written by Jerry Belson, Brock Yates
Directed by Hal Needham
Starring Burt Reynolds, Jackie Gleason, Jerry Reed, Sally Field

Five years after missing out on production for *The Longest Yard*, Florida officials were ready to bend over backwards to please Burt Reynolds in supplying locations for *Smokey and the Bandit II*. Scouting for a bridge to blow up, the filmmakers were offered not one, but two Orlando bridges by officials willing to sacrifice both.

Mike Henry and Jackie Gleason

This sequel to the 1977 hit film reunites all of the major cast members, including Reynolds as the fast-talking, fast-driving Bandit and Jackie Gleason playing not one, but three different law-enforcement officers. Three years later, minus Reynolds, Gleason returned to Florida to make *Smokey and the Bandit-Part 3*. (No word on why the switch from Roman to Arabic numerals, but no one seemed to mind.)

SOMETHING WILD (Orion - 1986)

Tallahassee
Written by E. Max Frye
Directed by Jonathan Demme
Starring Melanie Griffith, Jeff Daniels, Ray Liotta

"You look out for that girl."
Double-edged warning from Melanie Griffith's mother to Jeff Daniels.

Although she had appeared in other movies such as *Body Double, Something Wild* is the film that really began Melanie Griffith's climb to stardom. She plays the sexy and dangerous Lulu, who takes straightlaced Jeff Daniels for the ride of his life.

Melanie Griffith and
Jeff Daniels

Outside a New York cafe, she offers him a ride back to his office, only to take him to her high-school reunion in Pennsylvania.

The movie is highly charged with sex and comedy, and takes a turn for violent with the arrival of Griffith's ex-con former boyfriend Ray Liotta. Then an unknown, Liotta's volatile performance was so convincing that he later had difficulty getting cast in other roles.

(See "On Location")

SPRING BREAK (Columbia - 1983)

Fort Lauderdale
Written by David Smilow
Directed by Sean Cunningham
Starring David Knell, Steve Bassett, Perry Lang, Paul Land

Movies are always a sign of the times. In 1960, *Where the Boys Are* told the story of four girls on spring break in Fort Lauderdale. The movie set a moralistic tone about what is proper (dancing) and what is improper (premarital sex). As a result of the movie, Fort Lauderdale became a spring break mecca.

Twenty-three years later, *Spring Break* told the story of four boys on spring break in Fort Lauderdale. This time the tone was blatantly hedonistic, featuring sex, wet t-shirts, and Penthouse Pet of the Year Corrine Alphen. This is exactly the type of behavior that led Fort Lauderdale to clamp down on spring breakers, effectively driving them north to Daytona Beach.

STICK (Universal - 1985)

Fort Lauderdale, Miami
Written by Elmore Leonard, Joseph Stinson
Directed by Burt Reynolds
Starring Burt Reynolds, Candice Bergen, George Segal, Charles Durning, Dar Robinson

Florida icons Burt Reynolds and novelist Elmore Leonard came together to make *Stick*. Reynolds directed and starred in the film and Leonard co-wrote the script, based on his own novel. Set and filmed throughout South Florida, Reynolds stars as an ex-con who works his way up through the ranks of a chain of criminals, looking to exact

Burt Reynolds and friends

revenge for a murdered friend.

By some strange coincidence, *Stick* employed a disproportionate number of celebrity daughters. The obvious one is love interest Candice Bergen, daughter of famed ventriloquist Edgar. Close observers, though, will see that Tricia Leigh Fisher makes her screen debut as Reynolds' daughter. In real life, she is the daughter of Eddie Fisher and Connie Stevens. Shirley MacLaine's daughter Sachi Parker also makes her screen debut in this movie, playing a barmaid.

(See "On Location")

THE STRANGE ONE (Columbia - 1957)

Winter Park
Written by Calder Willingham
Directed by Jack Garfein
Starring Ben Gazzara, George Peppard

Ben Gazzara and George Peppard make their film debuts in *The Strange One*, the story of a southern military academy and the sadistic nature in which older students haze the underclassmen. It was also the film debut for director Jack Garfein, who was best known as actress Carol Baker's boyfriend. Garfein, Gazarra and most of the cast re-create their roles from Calder Willingham's Broadway play *End As a Man*. Winter Park's Rollins College and the Stetson

Ben Gazzara and friend

University College of Law in St. Petersburg double
for the military academy.

STRANGER THAN PARADISE (Goldwyn - 1984)

Melbourne
Written and Directed by Jim Jarmusch
Starring John Lurie, Eszter Balint, Richard Edson

Richard Edson, Eszter Balint
and John Lurie

*S*tranger Than Paradise was
the hit of the Cannes film
festival, and made director
Jim Jarmusch an instant icon
of independent filmmaking. In
an unusual technique, the
scenes in the movie play in
single-camera shots, with no
conventional editing. The film
follows three offbeat characters
on a trip that meanders from
New York to Cleveland to Florida.
When they make it to Florida, the travelers find
only a broken promise of paradise. Funny, loopy
and at times confusing, *Stranger Than Paradise* is
worth seeing if for no other reason than its non-
traditional approach to storytelling.

STRATEGIC AIR COMMAND (Paramount - 1955)

Tampa, Plant City
Written by Valentine Davies, Beirne Lay, Jr.
Directed by Anthony Mann
Starring James Stewart, June Allyson

Like the story of Red Sox great Ted Williams, this
movie has James Stewart playing a baseball player who is called back to military duty to fly jets.

The baseball scenes were shot in Plant City, where the Cincinnati Reds hold their spring training.

Actual Reds players suited up for the game.

Military sequences were filmed at Tampa's MacDill Air Force Base. Because production took place during the Korean conflict, the base and set were under strict security; no visitors were allowed to watch the filming. The public responded well to the film, especially to

James Stewart

the exciting Technicolor-VistaVision footage of the jets in action.

(See "On Location")

SUMMER RENTAL (Paramount - 1985)

St. Petersburg, Madeira Beach
Written by Jeremy Stevens, Mark Reisman
Directed by Carl Reiner
Starring John Candy, Richard Crenna, Rip Torn

Like reading a book on the beach, *Summer Rental* provides light entertainment. It features John Candy as an air-traffic controller who goes on vacation to break free from the stress of his job. Instead, he meets only headache and frustration as all of his plans go wrong. The finale is a giant boating regatta, where Candy

John Candy

gets to race bad guy Richard Crenna.

TARZAN FINDS A SON! (MGM - 1939)

Silver Springs
Written by Cyril Hume
Directed by Richard Thorpe
Starring Johnny Weissmuller, Maureen O'Sullivan

"Me Tarzan. You Jane."

Oft-quoted line that is never uttered in any of the Tarzan movies.

Florida folklore has it that most of the Tarzan films were shot at Silver Springs, outside Ocala. There is also a story that the monkeys inhabiting the area are the offspring of a runaway troop used in filming one of the movies. While both of these sto-

Johnny Weissmuller and
Maureen O'Sullivan

ries are fun, odds are that neither of them has much basis in truth. In fact, most of the Tarzan films were shot around Southern California.

As characters, Tarzan and Jane present a problem similar to that of Mickey and Minnie Mouse. Because they are not married in the official sense of the word, they cannot have children without implying sexual intercourse out of wedlock. Which is why *Tarzan Finds a Son!*

This movie did actually do some filming in Silver Springs. As the title implies, Johnny Weissmuller and Maureen O'Sullivan literally find the orphaned boy, named Boy, who is played by Johnny Sheffield. The film was to be the last featuring Maureen O'Sullivan, but the end was re-shot to bring her back to the jungle for...

TARZAN'S SECRET TREASURE (MGM - 1941)

Silver Springs
Written by Myles Connolly, Paul Gangecin
Directed by Richard Thorpe
Starring Johnny Weismuller, Maureen O'Sullivan

A nother Tarzan adventure that shot scenes at Silver Springs, *Tarzan's Secret Treasure* was the last to pair stars Johnny Weissmuller and Maureen O'Sullivan in the jungle. They reappeared together in *Tarzan's New York Adventure*, then O'Sullivan left to raise her children (among them Mia Farrow) and Weissmuller left MGM to make six more Tarzan films for RKO.

An interesting footnote to the Tarzan series are the two African tribes that go to war in nearly every film: The "Gibboneys" were named for studio art director Cedric Gibbons, and the "Joconeys" in honor of production head Joe Cohn. Although the tribes appear in a number of the Tarzan films, most of the footage had been shot for the 1931 film *Trader Horn*.

THEY WERE EXPENDABLE (MGM - 1945)

Key Biscayne
Written by Frank Wead
Directed by John Ford
Starring John Wayne, Donna Reed, Robert Montgomery, Ward Bond

T oward the end of World War II, director John Ford and actor Robert Montgomery took leaves of absence from the Navy to make this movie, based on the real exploits of a Navy torpedo boat in the Philippines during the early stages of the war. John Wayne was especially sensitive about portraying a war hero, because he had failed to qualify for military service due to his family, his age, and an old football shoulder injury.

The filming entailed notable difficulties. During

one battle scene, a windshield that was supposed to be made of safety glass was made of regular glass. When strafed with ball-bearing bullets, the glass exploded into Wayne's face. The Duke tried to duke it out with the technicians responsible, and Ford intervened. The two almost got into a fistfight before cooler heads prevailed.

John Wayne, Donna Reed and Robert Montgomery

Ford wasn't so lucky later in the production—he fell off a scaffold and broke his leg. With Ford immobilized, actor Montgomery directed the final two weeks of the shooting.

The real-life people portrayed by Wayne and Donna Reed proved they weren't so expendable after all. They sued MGM for unfair depiction and were awarded $3,000 and $290,000, respectively.

(See "On Location")

30 SECONDS OVER TOKYO (MGM - 1944)

Fort Walton Beach, Eglin Air Force Base
Written by Dalton Trumbo
Directed by Mervyn LeRoy
Starring Spencer Tracy, Van Johnson, Robert Walker, Robert Mitchum

At first Spencer Tracy didn't want to portray war hero Jimmy Doolittle in this movie about Doolittle's famous Tokyo Raid. But he took the part in order to boost the career of friend Van Johnson.

In the actual raid, sixteen B-25s flew from the deck of the USS *Hornet* to bomb Tokyo and other distant Japanese targets. Without enough fuel to return to the aircraft carrier, the planes had to land in China, leaving the crews to fend for themselves. Remarkably, most survived. One of the survivors was pilot Ted Lawson, whose leg had to be amputat-

Spencer Tracy

ed after a crash landing. While recuperating, he wrote the novel from which the film was made; Johnson portrays him in the film.

Filming at the air base was done on the same field that the real Doolittle used to train his raiders. During production, hostility erupted between the sometimes rowdy actors and the actual wartime air-corps personnel with whom they shared the base.

Director Mervyn LeRoy was none too thrilled at a mistake he made when he radioed a command to a B-25 squadron leader. Trying to complete a shot, he told the pilot to "Bring them in while the sun's still out." The command mistakenly blared in control towers throughout Florida, leaving the air-traffic controllers more than a little confused.

(See "On Location")

THIS IS CINERAMA (Cinerama - 1952)

Cypress Gardens
Developed by Fred Waller
Produced by Merian C. Cooper
Narrated by Lowell Thomas

One can only assume that audiences were starved for entertainment in 1952, because the top grossing film of the year was a technical sampler called *This Is Cinerama*. It's even more amazing when you consider that only forty-seven movie theaters in the world had the facilities to exhibit the film. It's a travelogue designed to highlight the vast visual scope that can be achieved with the wide-screen Cinerama process.

Cinerama achieves its effect by using three cameras, and later three projectors, working simultaneously to present a giant image. The idea is that the effect will make you feel you are actually experiencing what you see. This was particularly true of a segment filmed from the front of a roller coaster. One of the stops on the travelogue is Florida's Cypress Gardens.

After seeing the film, MGM boss Louis B. Mayer compared its impact to *Birth of a Nation*, which had convinced him to become a producer in 1915. He agreed to join Cinerama Corporation as a producer, and this eventually led to the 1962 MGM-Cinerama film *How the West Was Won*. But the process was too cumbersome to catch on and was short-lived.

TONY ROME (Fox - 1967)

Miami Beach
Writen by Richard L. Breen
Directed by Gordon Douglas
Starring Frank Sinatra, Jill St. John, Gena Rowlands

The complex—some would say confusing—*Tony Rome* starred Frank Sinatra as a hard-boiled detective hired to look into the doings of a millionaire's daughter. The film created a mini-industry for Sinatra in Miami.

Almost all of *Tony Rome*, and its sequel *Lady in Cement*, was shot at well-known Miami landmarks. Originally scheduled for ten weeks of shooting, production went off without a hitch and was completed three weeks early, even though Sinatra spent his nights doing a one-man show at the Fountainebleu.

TWELVE O'CLOCK HIGH (Fox - 1949)

Fort Walton Beach, Eglin Air Force Base
Written by Sy Bartlett, Beirne Lay, Jr.
Directed by Henry King
Starring Gregory Peck, Dean Jagger, Gary Merrill

Fox chairman Darryl F. Zanuck desperately wanted Gregory Peck to star in his wartime drama *Twelve O'Clock High*. But Peck rejected the script because he thought it was too much like MGM's star-filled flop *Command Decision*. A year later, Zanuck offered him the role again, with a unique resolution to the problem: In *Command Decision*, the big-name cast had actually detracted from the story. To counter that, the *Twelve O'Clock* cast would be unknowns. Peck agreed, and it turned out to be a wise decision.

Gregory Peck and friend

The film is based on the true story of Major General Frank Armstrong, and offers an unglamorized view of war. As commander of the Eighth Air Corps in England, Peck is forced to send an endless succession of pilots to certain death. This weighs on him and he eventually suffers a nervous breakdown. Peck recieved an Oscar nomination and won the New York Film Critics Award for Best Actor. Dean Jagger did him one better by taking the Oscar for Best Supporting Actor.

The film was shot with full military cooperation at Eglin Air Force Base. But the Air Force refused the request for a pilot to perform a wheels-up belly landing of a B-17, even though more than twenty servicemen volunteered to do the trick.

If the aerial scenes look realistic, that's because many of them are taken from American and

German archival footage of the war. In America, the filmmakers found footage of a B-17 having its tail sheared off and crashing down onto Berlin. They later located German film of the same plane going down. Pieced together, they provide realism that Hollywood magic could never hope to duplicate.

(See "On Location")

TWO THOUSAND MANIACS! (Box Office Spectaculars - 1964)

St. Cloud
Written and directed by Herschell Gordon Lewis
Starring Connie Mason, Thomas Wood

Gore-meister Herchell Gordon Lewis directed *Blood Feast*, which has the dubious distinction of being the first splatter movie. He also wrote and directed *Two Thousand Maniacs!* The maniacs of the title are the spirits of Confederate soldiers who, 100 years after the Civil War, get revenge by dismembering Northerners on vacation in Florida. It's one of those sensitive "feel good" movies.

WHERE THE BOYS ARE (MGM - 1960)

Fort Lauderdale
Written by George Wells
Directed by Henry Levin
Starring George Hamilton, Dolores Hart, Paula Prentiss, Jim Hutton, Yvette Mimieux, Connie Francis

More than any other film, *Where the Boys Are* shows why cities want to be used as movie locations. The year after this film portrayed a group of college students cavorting during spring break, Fort Lauderdale became mecca to an endless

Paula Prentiss, Yvette Mimieux and Connie Francis

wave of teenage spenders.

More interesting than the plot are the real-life stories of the cast members. Dolores Hart became a nun. Paula Prentiss had a nervous breakdown and married Richard Benjamin. Connie Francis' father tried to have her committed. Yvette Mimieux was married to director Stanley Donen. Jim Hutton died much too young and never got to see his son Timothy win an Oscar.

Then there's Palm Beach's George Hamilton. In addition to acting, he has made a career out of being a personal escort to LBJ's daughter and to Elizabeth Taylor, not to mention being the tannest man in the universe.

WHERE THE BOYS ARE '84 (ITC - 1984)

Fort Lauderdale
Written by Stu Krieger, Jeff Burkhart
Directed by Hy Averback
Starring Lisa Hartman

Although the plot of 1960's *Where the Boys Are* isn't much, it looks like a masterpiece when put up against its 1984 remake. Both films follow four college girls to Fort Lauderdale for spring break. But, oh what a difference twenty-four years make.

In the original film, the oddball was the "loose" girl willing to "go all the way." In the remake, the oddball is the "good" girl who isn't out looking for sex. George Hamilton, Connie Francis and Paula Prentiss, from the original's cast, all wisely declined when the sequel's producer Alan Carr offered them roles in this film.

WILD HARVEST (Hollywood Artists - 1962)

Homestead
Written by Sid Harris
Directed by Jerry Baerwitz
Starring Dolores Faith, Dean Fredericks

Set in the San Joaquin valley, *Wild Harvest* is about an evil ranch foreman who brutalizes his female workers. Walter Winchell narrates the film, which is best remembered for the revenge the women exact with the use of pruning shears. It is not to be confused with the better-known 1947 film of the same name, starring Dorothy Lamour and Alan Ladd.

WIND ACROSS THE EVERGLADES (Warner Brothers - 1958)

Everglade
Written by Budd Schulberg
Directed by Nicholas Ray
Starring Christopher Plummer, Burl Ives, Gypsy Rose Lee, Emmett Kelly

Burl Ives and
Christopher Plummer

Turn-of-the-century conservationists battle real-estate developers and poachers in *Wind Across the Everglades,* which was directed by super-cool *Rebel Without a Cause* director Nicholas Ray. Among the Floridians involved in the project are the Sarasota Schulbergs (screenwriter Budd and producer Stuart) and famed clown Emmett Kelly. Look for Peter Falk in his film debut as the writer. For the movie, the city of Everglade was made to look like Miami when it was still a small town.

THE YEARLING (MGM - 1946)

Hawthorne, Ocala National Forest
Written by Paul Osborn
Directed by Clarence Brown
Starring Gregory Peck, Jane Wyman, Claude Jarman, Jr.

"The greatest motion picture ever made."

Quote from playwright Moss Hart used in advertising.

Gregory Peck and
Claude Jarman, Jr.

Filming Marjorie Kinnan Rawlings' classic novel of a boy and his fawn proved a difficult task for Metro-Goldwyn-Mayer. In 1941, MGM sent Spencer Tracy, Anne Revere and Claude Eckman to Rawlings country in Marion County, near Ocala.

The Florida wilderness was less than hospitable. Along with the usual excess of insects, the young boy and the fawns hit unexpected growth spurts that made film continuity impossible. Furthermore, Tracy, bored and restless, complained that he couldn't find a good bar, and he had numerous run-ins with director Victor Fleming. King Vidor replaced Fleming, only to see the entire project scrubbed with the outbreak of World War II.

Four years later, the intrepid studio returned to Marion County with a new cast, and made a film that exemplified MGM's glory days of the 1940s. The picture packed houses, winning rave reviews and seven Oscar nominations, including Best Picture, Best Director, Best Actor and Best Actress.

While the effort proved profitable for MGM, the filming wasn't so gracious to Florida. Word of the difficulties encountered on both shoots helped slow production throughout the state.

But the film stands as a great visual record of frontier Florida. The first Technicolor film shot in Florida, the lush cinematography of the Ocala National Forest won an Academy Award. The Cross Creek homestead where Rawlings wrote *The Yearling* was used as a location for the picture, and is presently a state historic site.

YELLOWNECK (Republic - 1955)

Orlando
Written by Nat S. Linden, John Hugh
Directed by John Hugh
Starring Lin McCarthy

In *Yellowneck*, a group of five Confederate deserters tries to make its way through the Everglades and on to Cuba. The film didn't make much noise outside Orlando, where it was shot and also held its world premier. Orlando filmmaker John Hugh co-wrote and directed the picture.

Hollywood EAST

ON LOCATION

"LOCATION IS NOT VACATION."

This film-community cliché accurately sums up the rigors of shooting a movie where the scenery is. After all, it's hard to enjoy the Florida weather when you're working eighteen-hour days, six days a week. But movie production companies still stream into the Sunshine State for a variety of reasons, ranging from lower production costs to never-before-seen locales.

While it's flattering to be immortalized on film, communities often find their daily life disrupted during production. Streets are closed, public buildings are commandeered and trucks haul equipment day and night. But there are rewards: Production crews pump thousands of dollars into the local economy, and the area usually gains positive publicity. For this reason, most Florida counties have their own film offices, which help coordinate permitting, location scouting and local accommodations.

Pinpointing the locations used in a movie can be difficult. There's nothing like the glamor of a movie to turn a local booster into a shameless liar. If James Dean had ever cruised through a gas station in Orlando, some people today would swear it was the main location in *Rebel Without a Cause*. And press clippings and studio histories often simply say a film was shot "in the Florida swamps."

This chapter highlights many of Florida's better-documented filming locations. It divides Florida into six sections: Northeast, Central, Gulf Coast, The Keys, Southeast and The Panhandle. They will direct you to some interesting, obvious and just plain bizarre places that have played a part in the movies. You can go on location to re-enact scenes from your favorite Florida films, and find film festivals, movie palaces and unusual memorabilia.

DAYTONA BEACH

Despite what people might tell you in Indianapolis, Daytona Beach is Speed City, USA. The Daytona International Speedway is home to the Daytona 500 and other international racing events. This is where Tom Cruise came to shoot *Days of Thunder*, which was filmed all over town and even included some ultra-cool beach driving. Other *Thunder* locations include The Daytona Beach Hilton, Sophie Kay's Restaurant, The Broadway Bridge and Florida Health Care on Route 1.

GAINESVILLE

This sprawling, laid-back city in the heart of North Florida is home to the University of Florida. Although *Parenthood* was filmed mostly in Orlando, some scenes for the movie were shot on campus. The principal's office was set inside the university's Norman Hall. During Steve Martin's daydream, his son graduates on campus and then turns into a psychotic sniper, shooting from Century Tower in the heart of campus.

Mary Steenburgen in
Cross Creek

HAWTHORNE

The countryside around Hawthorne still retains the rustic charm Marjorie Kinnan Rawlings fell in love with in the '20s. Both *The Yearling* and *Cross Creek* were filmed at Marjorie Kinnan Rawlings' house on Route 3. The house is now a state historic site. Tours are offered every day except Tuesday and Wednesday.

JACKSONVILLE

Jacksonville may no longer be "The Winter Film Capital of the World," but the city has managed to make it into a few, albeit somewhat obscure, movies. Such is the case with *The Jacksonville Story*, a '50s documentary of life in the city. During the height of the Cold War, this 16mm film was shown to thousands of Soviets, who were amazed to see the inner workings of an actual American city.

Recent productions include Brooke Shield's un-released *Brenda Starr* and the kid-pic *The New Adventures of Pippi Longstocking*. Turner Network Television filmed *Orpheus Descending* at the local public television studio. Jacksonville and neighboring Ponte Vedra Beach doubled for Palm Beach in the television movie *The Prize Pulitzer*, which starred singer Chynna Phillips as Roxanne Pulitzer.

Movie Fans Won't Want to Miss...

The Florida Theater, located on Forsyth Street. The movie palace survives as an arts center, and hosts the annual Florida Film Festival at Jacksonville.

MICANOPY

This tiny town's main business is antiques—in fact, Micanopy itself seems untouched by time. *Cross Creek* was filmed throughout Micanopy's historic district, which is centered around the intersection of Cholokka Boulevard and Ocala Street. The hotel in the film is a building that's now called the Bay Tree Annex.

More recently, the historic district starred as Grady, South Carolina, "Squash Capital of the South," in the Michael J. Fox movie *Doc Hollywood*. The hospital where Fox works is an antique store called House of Hirsch. The parade and squash festival were held on Cholokka Boulevard, and starred many locals as extras. Unable to find a cafe in town, the production team built one for the picture, but dismantled it after filming.

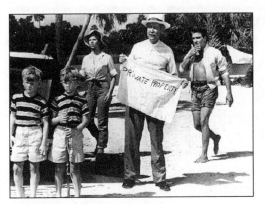

Elvis in *Follow That Dream*

OCALA

As the center of Florida's thoroughbred country, Ocala is well-served by financial institutions. Apparently, Elvis's bank of choice was Sun Bank, located on Silver Springs Boulevard downtown. It was used as a location in the movie *Follow That Dream,* in which the King played a squatter. No word on whether the bank guards were required to announce that "Elvis has left the building" upon his departure.

ST. AUGUSTINE

The nation's oldest city, St. Augustine has historic buildings that make it a location scout's delight. The

Gary Cooper in *Distant Drums*

most notable landmark is Castillo de San Marcos. This Spanish fort was used prominently in the Gary Cooper movie *Distant Drums*, and can be seen in Rob Lowe's disastrous *Illegally Yours*. Other locations for *Illegally Yours* include the Bridge of Lions and the Fountain of Youth.

The city also provided the backdrop for the 1915 silent classic *A Fool There Was*, based on the Kipling poem "The Vampire." It was the film debut for vamp actress Theda Bara. Just south of town is Marineland, which gets pillaged by an energetic man-fish during *Revenge of the Creature*. The Tragedy in U.S. History Museum features the car that was reduced to Swiss cheese in the final scenes of the movie *Bonnie and Clyde*.

SILVER SPRINGS

Because of its crystal-clear waters and exotic foliage, Silver Springs, outside of Ocala, has made its way into more films than any other Florida venue. It served as a hangout for swinger Johnny Weissmuller in *Tarzan Finds a Son!* and *Tarzan's Secret Treasure*. The springs also hosted *The Barefoot Mailman*, starring Robert Cummings, *Blindfold*, starring Rock Hudson and Claudia Cardinale, the Gary Cooper Indian picture *Distant Drums*, *The Yearling*, *Cross Creek*, *Creature from the Black Lagoon* and *Revenge of the Creature*. Attraction officials even claim to have hosted some of *Rebel Without a Cause*. A handout at the information desk directs you to specific locations.

Silver Springs was also the site of the world's first underwater film premiere. (See Weeki Wachee for the second.) RKO boss Howard Hughes premiered the film *Underwater* at the springs, 13 feet beneath the surface in a lake bed.

TRAL

Cape Canaveral
Cypress Gardens
Lakeland
Mount Dora
Orlando
Sanford

CAPE CANAVERAL

This sizable, mostly deserted, beach is best known as the location of the Kennedy Space Center. Although it has been a setting in numerous movies and in the television series *I Dream of Jeannie*, there hasn't been too much film production in and around the Space Center. After all, they're too busy launching real rockets to take time for fake ones.

Some movies have shot second-unit footage at the Cape, including Gregory Peck's *Marooned*, *The Right Stuff* and *Space Camp*. *The Right Stuff* was expected to do extensive location work in the area. But the overdeveloped coastline made it too difficult to find a stretch of beach that looked like it had in the 1960s.

CYPRESS GARDENS

With its water skiers, Southern belles and beautiful tropical foliage, Cypress Gardens was Florida's first theme park. It was also the main setting for the Esther Williams swim-tacular *Easy to Love*. For the movie, a 100-foot-long swimming pool was built in the shape of Florida. (Park officials named another pool after Williams.) An extra parking lot had to be constructed to handle all the tourists who came to watch filming. The gardens also provided a backdrop for *This Is Cinerama*, and second-unit scenes for the Betty Grable and Don Ameche film *Moon Over Miami*.

LAKELAND

Lakeland and its pastoral neighboring communities are best suited to playing small towns such as the one in *China Moon*. Filming for the Kevin Costner-produced movie included the Rath House in Bartow and a Winter Haven restaurant called Sally's Shrimp House. A Bartow house also doubled for the funeral home in the Macaulay Culkin film *My Girl*. Lakeland can been seen as the backdrop for the HBO movie *Sacrament*, starring Keith Carradine.

Movie Fans Won't Want to Miss...

The Polk Theater on Florida Avenue. This movie palace is open for special events, such as a gathering of three original Munchkins for a fiftieth anniversary screening of *The Wizard of Oz*. You can read Elvis Presley's autograph on the wall of the theater's dressing room—he appeared there in concert in 1956.

MOUNT DORA

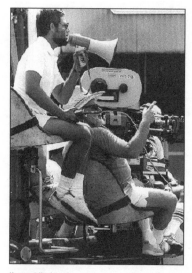

Howard Koch and John Schlesinger direct *Honky Tonk Freeway*

A sleepy, genteel village, Mount Dora is the opposite of tacky Ticlaw, the tourist-hungry town it played in *Honky Tonk Freeway*. But you still might find a few pink "Where the Hell is Ticlaw" T-shirts if you visit. Their color comes from the fact that the town in the film is painted pink to help attract tourists. Mount Dora business leaders were persuaded to let parts of the town be painted Pepto-Bismol style by the promise that their businesses would be freshly repainted whatever color they wanted after filming. A primary location used in the film is the turn-of-the-century Lakeside Inn, located on South Alexander Street.

ORLANDO

Slowly but deliberately, the city of Orlando is developing its image as Movieland South. Since winning both the Disney/MGM Studios and Universal Studios, Orlando has begun to challenge Miami as the state's filming center. Though the "studios" are still, for the most part, amusement parks, filming has been done on the sound stages and backlots there, as well as on location all over town.

DISNEY/MGM STUDIOS

Animators at Disney/MGM made ten minutes of magic for *Beauty and the Beast*. They also made the Roger Rabbit short *Roller Coaster Rabbit* and did extensive animation for the upcoming *Aladdin*. The studio's cutaway of a Delta L-1011 is one of the best airplane sets on the East Coast, which is why it was used to shoot principal interiors in *Passenger 57*, and the final scene of the Bill Murray movie *Quick Change*. The backlot was also used in a couple of scenes for the Disney film *Honey, I Blew Up the Kid*. The Sidney Poitier television movie *Separate But Equal* filmed its Supreme Court scenes on one of the studio's sound stages.

Ron Howard directs Rick Moranis and Steve Martin in *Parenthood*

UNIVERSAL STUDIOS

Universal has provided sound stages and its backlot for big-budget films like *Parenthood, Problem Child 2, Oscar* and the upcoming *Matinee*, produced by Steven Spielberg. The studio has also hosted the cable-television movies *Somebody Has to Shoot the Picture* and *Psycho IV*, and the television series *The Adventures of Superboy, Swamp Thing* and *Super Force*. Kids are familiar with Universal Studios as the home of the Nickelodeon cable network.

The studio has a "boneyard," an open area used to house large movie props after productions wrap, or close. Among the production souvenirs in the Universal boneyard is the houseboat used in the finale of *Cape Fear*. A wall alongside sound stage 21 is covered with plaques commemorating various productions filmed at the studio. (Intrepid visitors can locate a plaque for *King's Ransom*, which I co-wrote with Paul Stubenrauch.)

ORLANDO MOVIES

D.A.R.Y.L.

D.A.R.Y.L. is the story of a robot boy built by the government and placed in the care of a Norman Rockwell-style American family. The family's idyllic neighborhood is Euclid Avenue, in Orlando's historic Lake Cherokee section. When he wasn't at home, Daryl attended the Barkenton School, played by Kaley Elementary, on Kaley Avenue. Other locations featured in the film include Delaney Park and the East-West Expressway.

ERNEST SAVES CHRISTMAS

Bess Armstrong and Dennis Quaid in *Jaws 3-D*

This is a rare example of a movie that is actually set in Orlando. The stage work for the film was shot at the Disney/MGM Studios. The film's action opens at the Orlando International Airport. The Children's Museum in the film is actually the Orlando Science Museum in Loch Haven Park. Ernest's house is located on North Hyer Street.

JAWS 3-D

Most of *Jaws 3-D* is set at Orlando's Sea World, although the plot never explains how a shark can attack a city sixty miles from the ocean. The film exploits many of the park's attractions. But the underwater viewing station in the movie, searched for by many Sea World visitors, was just a set created for the film.

MY GIRL

Unable to secure stage space at Universal or Disney/MGM, this coming-of-age film starring Jamie Lee Curtis, Dan Aykroyd and Macaulay Culkin shot interiors at an empty warehouse off International Drive, Orlando's main tourist drag. Locations throughout Central Florida portrayed Madison, Pennsylvania, in the film. These include the towns of Sanford and Bartow, the Ocoee Christian Church, Old Plant City High School and Mirror Lake, near Clermont.

Steve Martin in *Parenthood*

PARENTHOOD

Orlando substitutes for St. Louis in this glimpse of middle-American family life. The opening scenes at a Cardinals' game were filmed at Tinker Field, home of the Southern League's AA Sun Rays. Steve Martin and Mary Steenburgen's house is on Lakeside Drive, near Leu Gardens, and his office is in the Landmark I building on Robinson, across from Lake Eola downtown. Rick Moranis sings "Close to You" to his wife at Howard Middle School, a historic landmark. Like some tourists, Martin and Steenburgen wreck their car on International Drive.

PROBLEM CHILD 2

Like *Parenthood*, *Problem Child 2* is a Universal picture that takes advantage of Orlando's studio and area without being set there. Parts of the movie were shot in downtown Orlando, where star Larraine Newman could be seen strolling in a pink bathrobe between takes. The food fight took place at The Bubble Room Restaurant on U.S. Highway 17-92, north of town— a location even more bizarre than the scene itself.

Movie Fans Won't Want to Miss...

Enzian Theater and The Hard Rock Cafe. The annual Florida Film Festival at Orlando is held at Enzian Theater, which Jamie Lee Curtis called "The Greatest Movie House Ever" when she was in town filming *My Girl*—you can read where she wrote it above the bar. Unlike most art-house cinemas, this one features a full dining menu.

The Hard Rock Cafe, located alongside Universal Studios, showcases mainly rock-and-roll memorabilia. But it has a room devoted to filmmaking, and its balcony offers a splendid view of the reconstructed *Psycho* house. Included in the movie memorabilia are Anthony Perkin's knife from the original *Psycho*, costumes worn by Laurel and Hardy in the movie *Jitterbugs* and the toboggan and autographed script from the Beatles movie *Help!* There is also a framed letter signed by cast and crew of *The Misfits*, including Marilyn Monroe, Montgomery Clift, Clark Gable and John Huston.

SANFORD

This small, lakeside "everytown," northeast of Orlando, was featured in three major movies in the course of one year. It doubled for downtown Madison, Pennsylvania in *My Girl*. It was also tapped for the Wesley Snipes film *Passenger 57* and the upcoming Dennis Quaid and Debra Winger movie *Wilder Napalm*. Many of the shooting locations are in or near the historic district; *Passenger 57* was filmed at the Sanford airport and at a traveling carnival hired for the movie.

GULF COAST

Clearwater
Plant City
St. Petersburg
Sarasota
Tampa
Tarpon Springs
Weeki Wachee
Wesley Chapel

CLEARWATER

Straddling a narrow peninsula, north of St. Petersburg, Clearwater boasts the studios of the Home Shopping Network, which may make it the most continuously televised city in the world. At the airport, you can see the hangars that served as sound stages for filming night scenes of the boat in *Cocoon*.

PLANT CITY

The baseball scenes at the beginning of *Strategic Air Command* were filmed in Plant City, the spring training home of the Cincinnati Reds. But star Jimmy Stewart is no Red in this pic, and he proves it by joining the fight to rid the world of communism.

John Candy in *Summer Rental*

ST. PETERSBURG

This retirement haven provides an appropriate setting for *Cocoon*, which filmed scenes all over town. Wilford Brimley gets rejected for his driver's license at the St. Petersburg Municipal Building, and the whole gang goes ballroom dancing at the St. Petersburg Coliseum on Fourth Avenue. In real life, the Coliseum's fine hardwood floor makes it a popular local dance spot.

The neighboring beaches have also been featured in various films. The grand Don Cesar Hotel, on Gulf Boulevard in St. Petersburg Beach, was the setting for Robert Altman's *Health*. Just north, in Madeira Beach, John Candy bumbled through *Summer Rental*.

More recently, *Coupe de Ville* was shot around town, including visits to Derby Lanes and the St.

Petersburg Kennel Club. *Lethal Weapon 3* filmed the implosion of the Soreno building, across the street from the St. Petersburg Municipal Marina.

SARASOTA

More than just the city where Pee Wee Herman was arrested at an adult theater, Sarasota is also the long-time winter home of the Ringling Brothers Barnum and Bailey Circus. That's why the movie *Dumbo* has its opening set in Sarasota, but since it was an animated feature, no camera crews needed to film in town. Cameras did roll for *The Greatest Show on Earth*, which made Sarasota its primary location. There are still some locals in town who performed in the film.

Movie Fans Won't Want to Miss...

The annual Sarasota French Film Festival and the Sarasota Opera House. The festival attracts big-name French filmmakers and stars. The foyer of the opera house sports a crystal chandelier from *Gone With the Wind*.

TAMPA

This Bay City East has the state's longest history in the movies, beginning in 1898 with the newsreels *U.S. Cavalry Supplies Unloading at Tampa Florida* and *Transport Ships at Port Tampa*, and continuing through the upcoming film *Cop and a Half*, starring Burt Reynolds. Tampa was also host to the first major studio film shot in Florida, the 1930 United Artists picture *Hell Harbor*.

DREW FIELD AND MACDILL AIR FORCE BASE

The military establishment openly courted Hollywood during the early days of World War II. The cast and crew of *Air Force* spent eight weeks filming at Drew Field. The military assisted in all phases of production, with two stipulations: that the film not give away any secrets of the featured B-17s, and that actual American servicemen not play the parts of enemy forces in the movie.

The Spencer Tracy classic *A Guy Named Joe* filmed at Drew Field and MacDill Air Force Base. Later, Jimmy Stewart went to MacDill to film military sequences for *Strategic Air Command*.

TAMPA MOVIES

BLACK LIKE ME

Tampa's historic Ybor City provided locations for this socially-conscious movie starring James Whitmore. The film was shot along Central Avenue and Cass Street and at one of the local beaches.

COCOON

Although it is set in St. Petersburg, *Cocoon* came to Tampa to film the famous scene in which Don Ameche break-dances. It was shot at a nightclub across the street from the University of South Florida.

Movie Fans Won't Want to Miss...

The Tampa Theater, which is located downtown on Franklin Street. The granddaddy of Florida movie palaces, this magnificent theater was designed by John Eberson. Unlike the other remaining movie palaces in the state, this one shows a regular schedule of movies and operates as an arthouse cinema.

Ron Howard directs Maureen Stapleton, Don Ameche and Hugh Cronyn in *Cocoon*

TARPON SPRINGS

This Greek community still thrives on the sponge-diving industry highlighted in *Beneath the 12 Mile Reef*. Most of the Tarpon Springs filming took place along the sponge docks on Dodecanese Boulevard.

Esther Williams

WEEKI WACHEE

Home to performing mermaids, the Florida landmark called Weeki Wachee lies at the intersection of Highways 19 and 50. This is where Esther Williams filmed *Neptune's Daughter*. The underwater theater hosted the world premiere of Don Knotts' movie *The Incredible Mr. Limpett*.

WESLEY CHAPEL

The horizon-hugging sameness and simplicity of the homes in the Carpenter's Run tract near here cried out to director Tim Burton for a paintbox color scheme. He obliged in *Edward Scissorhands*, topping off the effect with giant topiary accents.

THE KEYS

Key Biscayne
Key Largo
Key West
Little Palm Island

KEY BISCAYNE

Just a few decades ago, tony Key Biscayne could pass for an uninhabited Pacific island, complete with giant coconut trees. That's why John Ford selected it for the World War II classic *They Were Expendable*. This film about naval patrol boats in the Philippines shot all over the island and at the U.S. Coast Guard Station. The island has also seen the production of Esther Williams's *On an Island With You* and *The Barefoot Mailman*.

KEY LARGO

Although it is the namesake setting for the classic film, Key Largo itself made it into the film only as a second-unit location. However, while he was working on the script, John Huston stayed (and gambled) at the Caribbean Club, which is now a blue-collar bar.

Movie Fans Won't Want to Miss...

The African Queen. Because of his film *Key Largo*, Humphrey Bogart and the island have a nostalgic relationship of sorts. This may explain why the boat he piloted in *The African Queen* is housed at the Key Largo Holiday Inn, even though that picture filmed on location in Africa. Boat and hotel owner James Hendricks literally had to get an Act of Congress for permission to give tours on the boat. He has also acquired two boats used in the movie *On Golden Pond*.

KEY WEST

The end of the line for a lot of folks, Key West is the southernmost point in the contiguous forty-eight states, a fact that you're constantly reminded of when you visit there. Long a haven for artists and pirates, it has established a rogue identity in American films and literature.

While fishing here, director Howard Hawks bet Ernest Hemingway that he could make a good film from Hemingway's worst book. The result of the bet was *To Have and Have Not*, which was partially set in Key West, but shot at the Warner Brothers studio in Burbank.

Since the island's not too big, almost all the movies to visit it were filmed in the same general area in the heart of Old Key West. You can watch the sunset from Mallory Square like they do in *Running Scared*, or you can hang out on Smathers' Beach, where Robert Redford stands at the end of *Havana*.

A popular attraction is Ernest Hemingway's house, located at 907 Whitehead Street. It was featured prominently in the James Bond movie *Licence to Kill*. Hemingway's favorite hangout was the bar Sloppy Joe's. The original Sloppy Joe's is now Captain Tony's Saloon on Greene Street. A legend in the Keys, Captain Tony was played by Stuart Whitman in the movie *Cuban Connection*, which filmed scenes at the saloon. *Operation Petticoat* was shot at the submarine base, and *Beneath the 12 Mile Reef* filmed scenes on the local docks and at Fort Jefferson.

LITTLE PALM ISLAND

At Mile Marker 28.5 on Highway A1A, there is a ferry transfer from Little Torch Key to Little Palm Island, also called Munson Island. Now home to a luxury hotel, the island was once deserted enough to serve as a location for *PT-109*. One guest during filming was President John F. Kennedy, whose heroism during World War II inspired the film. Kennedy's visit was the reason that the island finally got electricity, water and telephone lines.

SOUTHEAST

BOCA RATON

How'd you like to live in a city whose English translation is "mouse mouth?" Actually quite a classy community, this is where Alan Alda tried his hand at quarterback in *Paper Lion*. Much of the film was shot at the St. Andrews Episcopal School for Boys. The real-life pros, mostly Detroit Lions and Miami Dolphins players, were paid a whopping $381 a week to take shots at Alda, who got paid considerably more. (Maybe that explains why they sometimes overdid it a little.) Scenes from Bette Middler's *Stella* and the Tom Selleck movie *Folks* were filmed at The Boca Raton Hotel and Club.

BRINY BREEZES

This quaintly-named trailer hamlet, located between Lantana and Delray Beach, has a population of only 300. Yet it was a primary location for the film *Folks*, starring Tom Selleck and Don Ameche. Since Briny Breezes is only two blocks long, you shouldn't have much trouble finding where they filmed.

DAVIE

The town of Davie was invaded by the filmmakers of *Caddyshack*, who took over the Rolling Hills Country Club. Chevy Chase and Rodney Dangerfield played golf, while groundskeeper Bill Murray blew up the place chasing after a lovable gopher.

FORT LAUDERDALE

Although famed hangouts like Penrods are gone, you can still travel Las Olas Boulevard and Highway

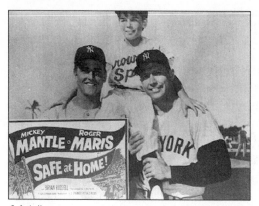

Safe At Home

A1A along the beach and see the shell of what was once spring break paradise, as featured in *Where the Boys Are*, *Where the Boys Are '84* and *Spring Break*. Some hangouts like The Candy Store are still around.

Fort Lauderdale doesn't want rowdy spring breakers anymore, but it's always willing to entertain production companies. This is where Mickey Mantle and Roger Maris stretched their acting abilities to play Mickey Mantle and Roger Maris in the 1962 film *Safe at Home*.

FORT LAUDERDALE INTERNATIONAL AIRPORT

Gonna fly now. The Fort Lauderdale airport has been used in a number of productions, sometimes subbing for Miami International, which is just too darn big and busy. Climactic scenes in *Married to the Mob* were filmed in Terminal 2 and at the Eastern ticket counter. Of course, Eastern is no longer with us, but through video we can remember. The airport also hosted *Folks*, *Revenge of the Nerds II* and *Police Academy 5: Assignment Miami Beach*.

FORT LAUDERDALE MOVIES

CAPE FEAR

Here are a few pointers for those of you who have yet to be frightened silly by the movie *Cape Fear*: Next time you attend a drama class at Broward Community College, don't suck on Robert De Niro's finger. Next time you stop at the Seminole Indian Truck Stop on North U.S. Highway 27, make sure there isn't a psychopathic killer lurking under your car. And whatever you do, if you're ever hiding behind a dumpster on Brickel Avenue and you hear someone call "Come out, come out, wherever you are," stay perfectly still.

TRACES OF RED

James Belushi, Lorraine Bracco and Tony Goldwyn were all over town for this 1992 film. Locations include the Monarch Galleries, Broward County Courthouse, St. Anthony's Catholic Church and Andy's Pub Too. The best treatment was given to the Squeeze nightclub—a Squeeze matchbook was used as a clue to the film's mystery.

Movie Fans Won't Want to Miss...

The Fort Lauderdale International Film Festival. This annual gathering is one of the largest film festivals and markets in the country.

HIALEAH

What you say? It's too hot to go to the beach. Why not play the ponies at the famed Hialeah racetrack. This is where Jon Voight played a has-been boxer/groom in the tearful movie *The Champ*.

HOLLYWOOD

Horray for Hollywood! This South Florida city has fought to maintain recognition for years, and even threatened legal suits when California's Hollywood tried to copyright the name. So, it's not surprising that nothing pleases locals more than stealing business from their famous cousin.

If you're looking for a night of passion, try starting with a stroll down the Hollywood Boardwalk. This is where Kathleen Turner led William Hurt astray in *Body Heat*. The truly daring can eat ice-cream cones along the way. The city's Hollywood

Boulevard played the main drag of the fictional town New Essex in *Cape Fear*. The ice cream store where De Niro stands outside, leaning on his car, is the Rainbo Cafe.

JUPITER

This is Burt Reynolds territory. You can even visit The Burt Reynolds Ranch, which is located two miles west of the Florida Turnpike on Jupiter Farms Road. Ranch highlights include a mini petting zoo, a feed store and a gift shop.

MIAMI

The Gold Coast has been a gold mine for film production from the earliest days of motion pictures. In 1919, D.W. Griffith came to Miami to direct *Jungle Trail*, at a Taj Mahal-like set built on Seybold Creek at Northwest 11th Street. Decades later, Don Johnson sped along these same streets in Miami Vice.

The city has also been successful at making cameo appearances in movies filmed elsewhere. Miami can be seen during a raid on Biscayne Bay in *Thunderball*, during the final scenes of the Tom Hanks movie *The Money Pit* and as second-unit footage when Cary Grant and Ingrid Bergman are driving at the beginning of Alfred Hitchcock's *Notorious*.

FOUNTAINEBLEU HOTEL

The Fountainebleu is to Miami Beach movies what Clint Eastwood is to spaghetti Westerns: You can't have one without the other. This is where Jerry Lewis is *The Bellboy* and James Bond's girlfriend gets

Frank Sinatra in *Tony Rome*

dipped in gold in *Goldfinger*. It's featured prominently in the Frank Sinatra movies *Tony Rome* and *Lady in Cement*. In real life, it's where Sinatra was served legal papers during the filming of *A Hole in the Head*. If all this is too much to resist, get right there.

THE ORANGE BOWL

No longer home to the Dolphins, the Orange Bowl is now the domain of the college-football powerhouse University of Miami Hurricanes, as well as the annual New Year's Day Orange Bowl game. The stadium played big roles in the Burt Reynolds comedy *Semi-Tough* and the disaster film *Black Sunday*.

VIZCAYA

This world-class mansion on Bayshore Drive was built by International Harvester magnate James Deering. It can be seen in numerous Miami movies, including *Absence of Malice, The Money Pit, Airport '77* and *Tony Rome*.

MIAMI MOVIES

ABSENCE OF MALICE

The fictional *Miami Standard* was actually in the *Miami Herald* building. Production took place between midnight and dawn, so as not to disrupt the newspaper.

CLAMBAKE

The grand finale of the movie occurs when Elvis races in the Orange Bowl Regatta, held at the Miami

Marine Stadium. The movie also filmed scenes at the Cape Florida Lighthouse, and features cool shots of the Miami skyline circa 1967.

THE GREATEST

Filming took place at Angelo Dundee's gymnasium and at a storefront mosque at 619 NW 2nd Avenue, where James Earl Jones, as Malcom X, converts Cassius Clay (Muhammad Ali) to Islam.

A HOLE IN THE HEAD

Frank Sinatra may have been staying at the Fountainebleu, but actual production on this screwball comedy took place at The Cardozo, located at 1300 Ocean Drive, Miami Beach. Sinatra takes a drive down Hotel Row on Collins Avenue, and a real-life court battle arose over scenes filmed at the West Flagler Kennel Club.

Dustin Hoffman and Jon Voight in *Midnight Cowboy*

MIDNIGHT COWBOY

At the end of the movie, the bus carrying Dustin Hoffman and Jon Voight pulls up along the Miracle Mile stretch in Coral Gables.

STICK

This Burt Reynolds film was shot throughout the Gold Coast. Famed stuntman Dar Robinson staged two falls from the twenty-story Grove Towers complex.

TONY ROME

Where didn't *Tony Rome* shoot in Miami? Most of the action takes place outdoors, at locations such as Mt. Sinai Hospital, Sip 'n Sup on the 79th Street

Causeway, Crandon Park Marina, Hotel Dolphin
and the Double Deck Turf Bar at the intersection of
NW 79th Street and 7th Avenue.

WHAT DO YOU SAY TO A NAKED LADY?

Eleven Miami co-eds stripped for this Alan Funt
feature that posed the title question to men faced
with the bare beauties. It is pretty much an extend-
ed and racier version of his television show *Candid
Camera* and radio show *Candid Microphone*. He sure
made a mint off one idea.

A complete list of the movies shot in Miami
would include the following:

ABSENCE OF MALICE (Columbia - 1981)
AIRPORT '77 (Universal - 1977)
AROUND THE WORLD UNDER THE SEA (MGM - 1966)
BAHAMA PASSAGE (Paramount - 1941)
BAND OF THE HAND (Columbia - 1951)
THE BELLBOY (Paramount - 1960)
BLACK SUNDAY (Paramount - 1977)
CEASE FIRE (Double Helix - 1985)
CLAMBAKE (United Artists - 1967)
COCOON: THE RETURN (20th Century-Fox - 1988)
DAY OF THE DOLPHIN (Avco Embassy - 1973)
DEEP THROAT (Arrow - 1972)
DON'T DRINK THE WATER (Avco Embassy - 1969)
FIRES WITHIN (MGM/Pathe - 1991)
FLIPPER (MGM - 1963)
THE GODFATHER, PART II (Paramount - 1974)
GOLDFINGER (MGM - 1964)
THE GREATEST (Columbia - 1977)
THE HAPPENING (Columbia - 1967)
THE HEARTBREAK KID (Fox - 1972)
HELLO DOWN THERE (MGM - 1969)
A HOLE IN THE HEAD (MGM - 1959)
HOW DO I LOVE THEE (ABC - 1970)
LADY IN CEMENT (Fox - 1968)

LENNY (United Artists - 1974)
MAKING MR. RIGHT (Orion - 1987)
MARRIED TO THE MOB (Orion - 1988)
THE MEAN SEASON (Orion - 1985)
MIAMI BLUES (Orion - 1990)
MIDNIGHT COWBOY (United Artists - 1969)
POPI (United Artists - 1969)
SCARFACE (Universal - 1983)
SEMI-TOUGH (United Artists - 1977)
SLATTERY'S HURRICANE (Fox - 1949)
STICK (Universal - 1985)
TONY ROME (Fox - 1967)

Movie Fans Won't Want to Miss...

The Gusman Cultural Center, a movie palace designed by John Eberson, which today hosts many events including the Miami Film Festival.

PALM BEACH

The city's namesake film, *The Palm Beach Story*, wasn't filmed in town. But this enclave, which has long been a caricature of dissolute wealth, is still the best place to shoot an exclusive area and stay in Florida. A number of the city's mansions are featured in films such as *Tony Rome*. The city also provided the backdrop for the Burt Reynolds television series *B.L. Stryker* and the upcoming James Belushi movie *Traces of Red*, which was filmed at the famed Breakers Hotel.

THE PANHANDLE

Eglin Air Force Base
Fort Walton Beach
Navarre Beach
Pensacola
Tallahassee
Wakulla Springs
Yankeetown

EGLIN AIR FORCE BASE

Spanning three counties, this sprawling military reservation near Pensacola hosted classic World War II films. *30 Seconds Over Tokyo*, starring Spencer Tracy and Van Johnson, filmed at the base's Hulbert Field. This was the actual area where Jimmy Doolittle trained pilots for the Tokyo raid that is featured in the film. The base also provided locations for the Gregory Peck film *Twelve O'Clock High*, which was nominated for Best Picture.

FORT WALTON BEACH

This hamlet's pristine beaches provided locations for Turner Network Television's turn-of-the-century film *Grand Isle*, based on Kate Chopin's novel *Awakening*.

NAVARRE BEACH

If you are swimming off the shore of this beach in Santa Rosa County and you hear deep, ominous music begin to play in the distance, get out of the water quick — this is where some of *Jaws 2* was filmed.

PENSACOLA

Surrounded by military bases, this Gulf-coast city has hosted a number of war movies. Pensacola recently was the filming site for the epic television mini-series *War and Remembrance*.
Movie Fans Won't Want to Miss...
The Saenger Theatre, a movie palace once known as "The Grand Dame of Palofax Place." The theater's

prize possession is a 1,000-pound Robert Morton theater organ named Lola.

TALLAHASSEE

Want to make Don Johnson jealous? Go swimming in the same pool that his wife Melanie Griffith used in the sexy comedy *Something Wild*. The pool's at the Tallahassee Motor Inn on North Monroe. Jeff Daniels goes incognito in a gift shop there in the same film. Exteriors were filmed in the nearby town of Quincy, in front of the Leaf Theater.

Even though *Something Wild* is supposed to take place in Pennsylvania, it contains a dead giveaway that filming was done in Tallahassee, home of the Florida State University Seminoles: As one scene begins, a truck passes by hauling a giant TV dish, with the Seminole team logo painted on it.

WAKULLA SPRINGS

Tucked on the outskirts of the Apalachicola National Forest, this rustic location was a fitting habitat for the *Creature from the Black Lagoon*, which was shot on location there. If you're brave enough to risk facing the Creature, you can take a little jungle cruise or stay at the park's cozy lodge. Call Wakulla Springs State Park for reservations.

YANKEETOWN

This tiny Southern beach town with the improbable name is where Elvis Presley filmed *Follow That Dream*, the story of a group of squatters who establish a waterfront homestead. Elvis and clan make their home alongside Yankeetown's Bird Creek Bridge.

Hollywood EAST

BEHIND THE SCENES

TANTALIZING TRIVIA

Want to impress strangers in those long movie
lines? Dream of talking your way onto a live
movie set? This chapter offers a lighthearted
look at quirky coincidences and little-known facts
that will give you the aura of a genuine movie
maven.

SECTION I – THE ULTIMATE FLORIDA MOVIE QUIZ

Pit your knowledge of Florida films against this
six-part mondo movie test. If you score an "A" on
this one, you need to get out of the theater and get a
little sun. For you folks who have a life, the answers
are listed at the end of the chapter.

PART I: The Sincerest Form of Flattery

**What actors portrayed the following real-life
individuals?**
1. War hero Jimmy Doolittle
2. Comedian Lenny Bruce
3. Writer George Plimpton
4. Key West Mayor Tony Tarracino
5. President John F. Kennedy

PART II: Tropical Debuts

Name the Florida films that provided these movie stars with their motion-picture debuts:
1. Faye Dunaway
2. Clint Eastwood
3. Peter Falk
4. Melanie Griffith
5. George Peppard
6. Paula Prentiss
7. Burt Reynolds
8. Lee Strasberg
9. Kathleen Turner

PART III: Separated at Birth

What does each series of films in the following list have in common?
1. *Cape Fear, The Champ, Scarface*
2. *Twelve O'Clock High, They Were Expendable, PT-109*
3. *The Greatest Show on Earth, Lenny, The Yearling*
4. *Easy to Love, Neptune's Daughter, On an Island With You*
5. *Blue City, Desperately Seeking Susan, Fires Within*
6. *Key Largo, The Right Stuff, Some Like It Hot*

PART IV: Chain of Hearts

Each of the following pairs of stars played opposite the same love interest in separate movies. Name the missing link and the films that are involved.
1. Paul Newman and Burt Reynolds
2. Steve Martin and Peter Coyote
3. Debra Winger and Bess Armstrong
4. Al Pacino and Alec Baldwin
5. Candice Bergen and Jill Clayburgh

PART V: Celluloid Sportsmen

In the following films, these actors portrayed professional athletes. Name the sport for each actor; as a bonus, name the particular position.

1. Burt Reynolds in *Semi-Tough*
2. Alan Alda in *Paper Lion*
3. Jon Voight in *The Champ*
4. Tom Cruise in *Days of Thunder*
5. Jimmy Stewart in *Strategic Air Command*

PART VI: All in the Family

Identify the real-life Hollywood family members who appeared in these Florida films:

1. The mother was in *Hello Down There*, the father in *Operation Petticoat* and the daughter in *My Girl*.

2. The husband was in *Cease Fire* and the wife in *Night Moves* and *Something Wild*.

3. One brother was in *Jaws 3-D* and *Wilder Napalm* and the other brother was in *Days of Thunder* and *Quick Change*.

4. The husband appeared in *Cross Creek* and *Summer Rental* and the wife appeared in *Honky Tonk Freeway*.

5. The mother co-starred in *Lady in Cement* and the daughter was an alien in *Cocoon*.

SECTION II – PEOPLE

The world of the movies is populated by bigger-than-life people. Filtered through publicity agents and magnified by the press, their personal lives become as fascinating as the roles they play. Some stars started out in Florida; others have gone there to lend their glamour and intrigue.

HOME-GROWN TALENT

These bright lights of the film industry all spent their formative years in the Sunshine State:

Brad Davis—This sensitive star of *Midnight Express* was one of a growing number of performers whose careers are cut short by AIDS. Fearful that he would be unable to get work, he kept his illness a secret until his death.

Jonathan Demme—This ultra-hip director/producer is responsible for films as diverse as *Melvin and Howard, Something Wild* and *Stop Making Sense*. He finally received well-deserved attention, and a Best Director Oscar, for *The Silence of the Lambs*.

Johnny Depp—After starring on the television series *21 Jump Street*, this actor fought being typecast as every teenage girl's dream. His breakthrough came in his home state, with Tim Burton's *Edward Scissorhands*.

Faye Dunaway—This Bascom native has starred in movies such as *Little Big Man, Chinatown, Three Days of the Condor, The Champ* and *Network*, for which she won an Oscar for Best Actress.

Stepin Fetchit—Born Lincoln Theodore Monroe Andrew Perry, he took his stage name after a race-horse he once won money betting on. This Key West native was the first African American to receive featured billing.

Veronica Lake—Known for her blond hair cascading over one eye, this '40s leading lady starred in *This Gun for Hire, Sullivan's Travels* and *Slattery's Hurricane,* which was filmed in her native Miami.

Butterfly McQueen—Famous for playing Prissy in *Gone With the Wind,* this actress is from Tampa.

Sidney Poitier—The great star of films like *Lilies of the Field, The Defiant Ones* and *Guess Who's Coming to Dinner* lived in the Bahamas but was born in Miami.

Burt Reynolds—Born in Waycross, Georgia, but raised in Jupiter, Burt Reynolds has done more to promote Florida production than any other film-maker. His Florida films include *Angel Baby, Semi-Tough,* the upcoming *Cop and a Half* and *Stick,* which he also directed.

Wesley Snipes—The present-day leading man of *Passenger 57, Jungle Fever, New Jack City* and *Mo' Better Blues* is a graduate of Orlando's Jones High School.

LOVE MEANS NEVER HAVING TO DO SEPARATE MOVIES

Florida has a reputation as a romantic vacation get-away, which may explain why these real-life couples made movies together in the Sunshine State (or, in some cases, met and fell in love there on the set).

Hume Cronyn and Jessica Tandy
Cocoon
Cocoon: The Return
Honky Tonk Freeway
Tom Cruise and Nicole Kidman
Days of Thunder
Johnny Depp and Winona Ryder
Edward Scissorhands
Vincent D'Onofrio and Greta Scacchi
Fires Within
Sterling Hayden and Madeleine Carroll
Bahama Passage
Richard Jordan and Blair Brown
A Flash of Green
Alex Karras and Susan Clark
Porky's
Malcolm McDowell and Mary Steenburgen
Cross Creek
Paul Newman and Joanne Woodward
Harry and Son

I KNOW WHO'D BE PERFECT FOR THE ROLE!

When pressed to find talent for a sports movie, does a casting director opt for an actor who can't play, or a player who can't act? In these cases, it was the latter. The following celebrities played themselves in Florida films:

Muhammad Ali
   The Greatest
Alex Karras
   Paper Lion
Joe Robbie
   Black Sunday
Mickey Mantle
   Safe at Home
Roger Maris
   Safe at Home
Carl Hubbell
   Big Leaguer

SPECIAL POWERS OF NON-HUMANS

In the world of the movies, aliens, animals and humanoids never get an even break, despite their obvious superiority. The following creatures all fall prey to jealous humans:

Name: Edward Scissorhands
Special skill: Cuts things
Falls in love with: Winona Ryder
Society's betrayal: Driven back to his castle to live alone

Name: D.A.R.Y.L.
Special skills: Baseball, video games
Falls in love with: Adoptive parents
Society's betrayal: Government tries to take him back

Names: Alpha and Beta (*Day of the Dolphin*)
Special skill: Talking
Fall in love with: George C. Scott
Society's betrayal: Trained to blow up President's
yacht

Name: The Yearling
Special skill: Destroying crops
Falls in love with: Claude Jarman, Jr.
Society's betrayal: Killed by owners

Name: Antereans (*Cocoon*)
Special skills: Skin peeling, eternal life
Fall in love with: Steve Guttenberg
Society's betrayal: Cocoon-disturbing

Name: Creature from the Black Lagoon
Special skills: Gill-breathing, eating people
Falls in love with: Julie Adams
Society's betrayal: Put on display at Marineland

Name: The Beast (*Beauty and the Beast*)
Special skills: Moping, talking dishware
Falls in love with: Belle
Society's betrayal: Castle stormed

Name: Ulysses (*Making Mr. Right*)
Special skills: Super-intelligent, no emotions
Falls in love with: Ann Magnuson
Society's betrayal: Plan to send him into deep space

SECTION III – PRODUCTION

It's been said that the thousands of movies that have been made share only seven different plots. After looking over this section, you may be inclined to agree.

THE LONG AND THE SHORT OF IT

Budget, running time, quality and profit vary wildy from film to film. Unfortunately, no one has ever found a correlation among them, which is why predicting a hit is still more art than science. Here are some wide-ranging statistics on Florida films:

Budget for *Gal Young Un*: **$94 thousand**
Budget for *Days of Thunder*: **$60 million**

Running time for *The Big Leaguer*: **70 minutes**
Running time for *Scarface*: **173 minutes**

Box-office earnings per production dollar on *Honky Tonk Freeway*: **$.02**
Box-office earnings per production dollar on *Deep Throat*: **$120,000**

LET'S DO IT AGAIN

If it ain't broke, don't fix it—just head to the Sunshine State and do it over easy. The following Florida films are all sequels:

AIRPORT '77
CADDYSHACK II
COCOON: THE RETURN
ERNEST SAVES CHRISTMAS
THE GODFATHER, PART II

GOLDFINGER
JAWS 2
JAWS 3-D
LADY IN CEMENT
LETHAL WEAPON 3
LICENCE TO KILL
POLICE ACADEMY 5:
     ASSIGNMENT MIAMI BEACH
PORKY'S 2
PORKY'S REVENGE
PROBLEM CHILD 2
REVENGE OF THE CREATURE
REVENGE OF THE NERDS 2: NERDS IN PARADISE
SMOKEY AND THE BANDIT II
SMOKEY AND THE BANDIT-PART 3
WHERE THE BOYS ARE '84

CLAMBAKE/DAYS OF THUNDER: Is It Real, or Is It Memorex?

Despite its reported $60 million budget and its original-story credit for Tom Cruise, the careful viewer will see that 1990's *Days of Thunder* is merely a rehash of the 1967 Elvis movie *Clambake*.

Clam: Chamber of Commerce dreams come true, as Sex God Elvis Presley poses next to Miami landmarks.

Days: Chamber of Commerce dreams come true, as Sex God Tom Cruise poses next to Daytona Beach landmarks.

Clam: Elvis falls in love with co-star Shelley Fabares, who is mostly known as the girl in the Elvis movies.

Days: Tom falls in love with co-star Nicole Kidman, who is mostly known as Mrs. Cruise.

Clam: Elvis must do battle with pretty boy Bill Bixby.

Days: Tom must do battle with pretty boy Cary Elwes.

Clam: Elvis doesn't sing too good in this one.
Days: Tom doesn't act too good in this one.
Clam: Grand finale is when Elvis races in the Orange Bowl Regatta.
Days: Grand finale is when Tom races in the Daytona 500.
Clam: Production is overseen by megalomaniac Colonel Tom Parker.
Days: Production is overseen by megalomaniacs Don Simpson and Jerry Bruckheimer.
Clam: Critics hate it.
Days: Critics hate it.
Clam: Audiences love it.
Days: Audiences love it.

WAR MOVIES FILMED IN FLORIDA

Perhaps some of Florida's most important roles have been in war movies. Many of these films were aimed at increasing the patriotism of American audiences during World War II, but settings have ranged from the Civil War to Vietnam.

AIR FORCE—World War II
CEASE FIRE—Vietnam
DISTANT DRUMS—Seminole Indian Wars
A GUY NAMED JOE—World War II
PT-109—World War II
SEMINOLE—Seminole Indian Wars
STRATEGIC AIR COMMAND—Korean conflict
THEY WERE EXPENDABLE—World War II
30 SECONDS OVER TOKYO—World War II
TWELVE O'CLOCK HIGH—World War II
YELLOWNECK—Civil War

THE ULTIMATE FLORIDA MOVIE QUIZ - ANSWERS

PART I

1. Spencer Tracy in *30 Seconds Over Tokyo*
2. Dustin Hoffman in *Lenny*
3. Alan Alda in *Paper Lion*
4. Stuart Whitman in *Cuba Crossing*
5. Cliff Robertson in *PT-109*

PART II

1. *The Happening*
2. *Revenge of the Creature*
3. *Wind Across the Everglades*
4. *Night Moves*
5. *The Strange One*
6. *Where the Boys Are*
7. *Angel Baby*
8. *The Godfather, Part II*
9. *Body Heat*

PART III

1. They're all remakes of other movies.
2. They're all World War II movies.
3. They were all nominated for Best Picture.
4. They all star Esther Williams.
5. They were all directed by women.
6. They were all set in Florida but filmed
   somewhere else.

PART IV

1. Sally Field—*Absence of Malice* and *Smokey and
   the Bandit II*
2. Mary Steenburgen—*Parenthood* and *Cross Creek*
3. Dennis Quaid—*Wilder Napalm* and *Jaws 3-D*
4. Michelle Pfeiffer—*Scarface* and *Married to the Mob*
5. Burt Reynolds—*Stick* and *Semi-Tough*

PART V

1. Football; Running Back
2. Football; Quarterback
3. Boxing
4. Auto Racing
5. Baseball; Third Base

PART VI

1. Janet Leigh, Tony Curtis and Jamie Lee Curtis
2. Don Johnson and Melanie Griffith
3. Dennis Quaid and Randy Quaid
4. Rip Torn and Geraldine Page
5. Raquel Welch and Tahnee Welch

Hollywood EAST

END CREDITS

FLORIDA FILM FAST FACTS

T he lists in this chapter provide facts-at-a-glance about specific Florida films, their makers and their eras. The films are organized by year, by city, by studio, by director and by actor. Academy Award nominees and winners are listed at the end.

FILM PRODUCTION BY YEAR

1930   HELL HARBOR

1939   TARZAN FINDS A SON!

1941   BAHAMA PASSAGE
       TARZAN'S SECRET TREASURE

1943   AIR FORCE

1944   A GUY NAMED JOE
       30 SECONDS OVER TOKYO

1945   THEY WERE EXPENDABLE

1946   THE YEARLING

1948   MR. PEABODY AND THE MERMAID
       ON AN ISLAND WITH YOU

1949   NEPTUNE'S DAUGHTER
       SLATTERY'S HURRICANE
       TWELVE O'CLOCK HIGH

1950   A LADY WITHOUT PASSPORT

1951   CROSSWINDS
       DISTANT DRUMS

1952   THE GREATEST SHOW ON EARTH
THIS IS CINERAMA

1953   BENEATH THE 12 MILE REEF
THE BIG LEAGUER
EASY TO LOVE
SEMINOLE

1954   CREATURE FROM THE BLACK LAGOON

1955   REVENGE OF THE CREATURE
THE ROSE TATTOO
STRATEGIC AIR COMMAND
YELLOWNECK

1957   THE STRANGE ONE

1958   WIND ACROSS THE EVERGLADES

1959   A HOLE IN THE HEAD
OPERATION PETTICOAT

1960   ANGEL BABY
THE BELLBOY
WHERE THE BOYS ARE

1962   ALL FALL DOWN
FOLLOW THAT DREAM
SAFE AT HOME
WILD HARVEST

1963   FLIPPER
PT-109

1964   BLACK LIKE ME
GOLDFINGER
TWO THOUSAND MANIACS!

1965   GIRL HAPPY

1966   AROUND THE WORLD UNDER THE SEA
BLINDFOLD
FAT SPY
JOHNNY TIGER

1967   CLAMBAKE
THE HAPPENING
TONY ROME

1968 LADY IN CEMENT
      PAPER LION

1969 DON'T DRINK THE WATER
      HELLO DOWN THERE
      MIDNIGHT COWBOY
      POPI

1970 HOW DO I LOVE THEE?

1972 DEEP THROAT
      THE HEARTBREAK KID

1973 THE DAY OF THE DOLPHIN

1974 THE GODFATHER, PART II
      LENNY

1975 NIGHT MOVES
      92 IN THE SHADE

1977 AIRPORT '77
      BLACK SUNDAY
      THE GREATEST
      SEMI-TOUGH

1978 JAWS 2
      THE NORSEMAN

1979 THE CHAMP
      GAL YOUNG UN
      HEALTH

1980 CADDYSHACK
      CUBA CROSSING
      SMOKEY AND THE BANDIT II

1981 ABSENCE OF MALICE
      BODY HEAT
      GHOST STORY
      HONKY TONK FREEWAY

1982 PORKY'S

1983   CROSS CREEK
        JAWS 3-D
        PORKY'S II: THE NEXT DAY
        SCARFACE
        SMOKEY AND THE BANDIT, PART 3
        SPRING BREAK

1984   A FLASH OF GREEN
        HARRY AND SON
        A NIGHT IN HEAVEN
        STRANGER THAN PARADISE
        WHERE THE BOYS ARE '84

1985   CEASE FIRE
        COCOON
        D.A.R.Y.L.
        THE MEAN SEASON
        PORKY'S REVENGE
        STICK
        SUMMER RENTAL

1986   BAND OF THE HAND
        BLUE CITY
        FLIGHT OF THE NAVIGATOR
        RUNNING SCARED
        SOMETHING WILD

1987   MAKING MR. RIGHT

1988   COCOON: THE RETURN
        ERNEST SAVES CHRISTMAS
        ILLEGALLY YOURS
        MARRIED TO THE MOB
        POLICE ACADEMY 5:
            ASSIGNMENT MIAMI BEACH

1989   LET IT RIDE
        LICENCE TO KILL
        PARENTHOOD
        RUDE AWAKENING

1990   COUPE DE VILLE
        DAYS OF THUNDER
        EDWARD SCISSORHANDS
        HAVANA
        MIAMI BLUES

1991   BEAUTY AND THE BEAST
        BRENDA STARR
        CAPE FEAR
        DOC HOLLYWOOD
        FIRES WITHIN
        MY GIRL
        OSCAR
        PROBLEM CHILD 2
        QUICK CHANGE

1992   CHINA MOON
        COP AND A HALF
        CRISSCROSS
        FOLKS
        LETHAL WEAPON 3
        MATINEE
        PASSENGER 57
        WILDER NAPALM

FILM PRODUCTION BY CITY

BARTOW
CHINA MOON
MY GIRL

BRADENTON
A FLASH OF GREEN

BOCA RATON
FOLKS
PAPER MOON
STELLA

BRINY BREEZES
FOLKS

CAPE CORAL
FAT SPY

CYPRESS GARDENS
EASY TO LOVE
MOON OVER MIAMI
THIS IS CINERAMA

DAVIE
CADDYSHACK
CADDYSHACK II

DAYTONA BEACH
DAYS OF THUNDER

DELAND
GHOST STORY

THE EVERGLADES
A LADY WITHOUT PASSPORT
THE MEAN SEASON
SEMINOLE
WIND ACROSS THE EVERGLADES

FORT LAUDERDALE
CAPE FEAR
DEEP THROAT
FLIGHT OF THE NAVIGATOR
GIRL HAPPY
HARRY AND SON
MARRIED TO THE MOB
PORKY'S
PORKY'S II: THE NEXT DAY
PORKY'S REVENGE
SAFE AT HOME
SPRING BREAK
STICK
WHERE THE BOYS ARE
WHERE THE BOYS ARE '84

FORT MYERS
A FLASH OF GREEN

FORT WALTON BEACH
30 SECONDS OVER TOKYO
TWELVE O'CLOCK HIGH

GAINESVILLE
DOC HOLLYWOOD
GAL YOUNG UN

HAWTHORNE
CROSS CREEK
THE YEARLING

HIALEAH
THE CHAMP
LET IT RIDE

HOLLYWOOD
BODY HEAT
CAPE FEAR

HOMESTEAD
ANGEL BABY
WILD HARVEST

HOMOSASSA SPRINGS
CROSSWINDS

JACKSONVILLE
BRENDA STARR

JUPITER
SMOKEY AND THE BANDIT II

THE KEYS
BLUE CITY

KEY BISCAYNE
ON AN ISLAND WITH YOU
THEY WERE EXPENDABLE

KEY WEST
ALL FALL DOWN
BENEATH THE 12 MILE REEF
CRISSCROSS
CUBA CROSSING
HAVANA
LICENCE TO KILL
92 IN THE SHADE
OPERATION PETTICOAT
THE ROSE TATTOO
RUNNING SCARED

LAKE WORTH
BODY HEAT

LAKELAND
CHINA MOON

LITTLE PALM ISLAND
PT-109

MADEIRA BEACH
SUMMER RENTAL

MARINELAND
REVENGE OF THE CREATURE

MELBOURNE
THE BIG LEAGUER
STRANGER THAN PARADISE

MIAMI
ABSENCE OF MALICE
AIRPORT '77
AROUND THE WORLD UNDER THE SEA
BAHAMA PASSAGE
BAND OF THE HAND
THE BELLBOY
BLACK SUNDAY
CEASE FIRE
CLAMBAKE
COCOON: THE RETURN
DAY OF THE DOLPHIN
DEEP THROAT
DON'T DRINK THE WATER
FIRES WITHIN
FLIPPER
THE GODFATHER, PART II
GOLDFINGER
THE GREATEST
THE HAPPENING
THE HEARTBREAK KID
HELLO DOWN THERE
A HOLE IN THE HEAD
HOW DO I LOVE THEE?
LADY IN CEMENT
LENNY
MAKING MR. RIGHT
MARRIED TO THE MOB
THE MEAN SEASON
MIAMI BLUES
MIDNIGHT COWBOY
POLICE ACADEMY 5: ASSIGNMENT MIAMI BEACH
POPI
SCARFACE
SEMI-TOUGH
SLATTERY'S HURRICANE
STICK
TONY ROME

MICANOPY
CROSS CREEK
DOC HOLLYWOOD

MOUNT DORA
HONKY TONK FREEWAY

NAPLES
THE BAREFOOT MAILMAN
DISTANT DRUMS

NAVARRE BEACH
JAWS 2

OCALA
BLINDFOLD
CREATURE FROM THE BLACK LAGOON
DISTANT DRUMS
FOLLOW THAT DREAM
REVENGE OF THE CREATURE
TARZAN FINDS A SON!
TARZAN'S SECRET TREASURE

OCALA NATIONAL FOREST
THE YEARLING

ORLANDO
BEAUTY AND THE BEAST
D.A.R.Y.L.
ERNEST SAVES CHRISTMAS
JAWS 3-D
LETHAL WEAPON 3
MATINEE
MY GIRL
OSCAR
PARENTHOOD
PASSENGER 57
PROBLEM CHILD 2
QUICK CHANGE
YELLOWNECK

PLANT CITY
MY GIRL
STRATEGIC AIR COMMAND

ST. AUGUSTINE
THE BAREFOOT MAILMAN
DISTANT DRUMS
ILLEGALLY YOURS

ST. CLOUD
TWO THOUSAND MANIACS!

ST. PETERSBURG
COCOON
HEALTH
LETHAL WEAPON 3
SUMMER RENTAL

SANFORD
MY GIRL
PASSENGER 57
WILDER NAPALM

SANIBEL ISLAND
NIGHT MOVES

SARASOTA
A FLASH OF GREEN
THE GREATEST SHOW ON EARTH

TALLAHASSEE
SOMETHING WILD

TAMPA
AIR FORCE
BLACK LIKE ME
COP AND A HALF
COUPE DE VILLE
A GUY NAMED JOE
HELL HARBOR
THE NORSEMAN
STRATEGIC AIR COMMAND

TARPON SPRINGS
BENEATH THE 12 MILE REEF

TITUSVILLE
A NIGHT IN HEAVEN

VENICE
A FLASH OF GREEN

WAKULLA SPRINGS
CREATURE FROM THE BLACK LAGOON

WEEKI WACHEE
MR. PEABODY AND THE MERMAID
NEPTUNE'S DAUGHTER

WEKIWA SPRINGS
JOHNNY TIGER
RUDE AWAKENING

WESLEY CHAPEL
EDWARD SCISSORHANDS

WINTER PARK
THE STRANGE ONE

YANKEETOWN
FOLLOW THAT DREAM

FILM PRODUCTION BY MAJOR STUDIO

COLUMBIA
ABSENCE OF MALICE - 1981
BAND OF THE HAND - 1986
THE GREATEST - 1977
THE HAPPENING - 1967
MY GIRL - 1991
SAFE AT HOME - 1962
SPRING BREAK - 1983
THE STRANGE ONE - 1957

DISNEY (including Touchstone)
BEAUTY AND THE BEAST - 1991
ERNEST SAVES CHRISTMAS - 1988
FLIGHT OF THE NAVIGATOR - 1986
OSCAR - 1991

MGM (including MGM/UA and MGM/Pathe)
AROUND THE WORLD UNDER THE SEA - 1966
THE BIG LEAGUER - 1953
THE CHAMP - 1979
CRISSCROSS - 1992
EASY TO LOVE - 1953
FIRES WITHIN - 1991
FLIPPER - 1963
GIRL HAPPY - 1965
GOLDFINGER - 1964
A GUY NAMED JOE - 1944
HELLO DOWN THERE - 1969
A LADY WITHOUT PASSPORT - 1950
LICENCE TO KILL - 1989
NEPTUNE'S DAUGHTER - 1949
ON AN ISLAND WITH YOU - 1948
RUNNING SCARED - 1986
TARZAN FINDS A SON! - 1939
TARZAN'S SECRET TREASURE - 1941
THEY WERE EXPENDABLE - 1945
30 SECONDS OVER TOKYO - 1944
WHERE THE BOYS ARE - 1960
THE YEARLING - 1946

ORION
CADDYSHACK - 1980
CADDYSHACK II - 1988
CHINA MOON - 1992
HARRY AND SON - 1984
MAKING MR. RIGHT - 1987
MARRIED TO THE MOB - 1988
THE MEAN SEASON - 1985
MIAMI BLUES - 1990
RUDE AWAKENING - 1989
SOMETHING WILD - 1986

PARAMOUNT
BAHAMA PASSAGE - 1941
THE BELLBOY - 1960
BLACK SUNDAY - 1977

BLUE CITY - 1986
CROSSWINDS - 1951
D.A.R.Y.L. - 1985
DAYS OF THUNDER - 1990
THE GODFATHER, PART II - 1974
THE GREATEST SHOW ON EARTH - 1952
LET IT RIDE - 1989
THE ROSE TATTOO - 1955
STRATEGIC AIR COMMAND - 1955
SUMMER RENTAL - 1985

TWENTIETH CENTURY-FOX
BENEATH THE 12 MILE REEF - 1953
COCOON - 1985
COCOON: THE RETURN - 1988
EDWARD SCISSORHANDS - 1990
HEALTH - 1979
THE HEARTBREAK KID - 1972
LADY IN CEMENT - 1968
A NIGHT IN HEAVEN - 1984
PORKY'S - 1982
PORKY'S II: THE NEXT DAY - 1983
PORKY'S REVENGE - 1985
SLATTERY'S HURRICANE - 1949
TONY ROME - 1967
TWELVE O'CLOCK HIGH - 1949

UNITED ARTISTS
CLAMBAKE - 1967
FOLLOW THAT DREAM - 1962
HELL HARBOR - 1930
A HOLE IN THE HEAD - 1959
LENNY - 1974
MIDNIGHT COWBOY - 1969
PAPER LION - 1968
POPI - 1969
SEMI-TOUGH - 1977

UNIVERSAL
AIRPORT '77 - 1977
BLINDFOLD - 1966
CAPE FEAR - 1991
COP AND A HALF - 1992
COUPE DE VILLE - 1990
CREATURE FROM THE BLACK LAGOON - 1954
GHOST STORY - 1981
HAVANA - 1990
JAWS 2 - 1978
JAWS 3-D - 1983
MATINEE - 1992
MR. PEABODY AND THE MERMAID - 1948
OPERATION PETTICOAT - 1959
PARENTHOOD - 1989
PROBLEM CHILD II - 1981
REVENGE OF THE CREATURE - 1955
SCARFACE - 1983
SEMINOLE - 1953
SMOKEY AND THE BANDIT II - 1980
STICK - 1985

WARNER BROTHERS
AIR FORCE - 1943
BODY HEAT - 1981
DISTANT DRUMS - 1951
DOC HOLLYWOOD - 1991
LETHAL WEAPON 3 - 1992
NIGHT MOVES - 1975
PASSENGER 57 - 1992
POLICE ACADEMY 5: ASSIGNMENT MIAMI
    BEACH - 1988
PT-109 - 1963
QUICK CHANGE - 1991
WIND ACROSS THE EVERGLADES - 1958

FILM PRODUCTION BY DIRECTOR

Robert Aldrich	THE BIG LEAGUER
Robert Altman	HEALTH
Joe Alves	JAWS 3-D
Alan Arkush	CADDYSHACK II
George Armitage	MIAMI BLUES
Gillian Armstrong	FIRES WITHIN
Jack Arnold	CREATURE FROM THE BLACK LAGOON, HELLO DOWN THERE, REVENGE OF THE CREATURE
Hy Averback	WHERE THE BOYS ARE '84
John Avildsen	A NIGHT IN HEAVEN
Jerry Baerwitz	WILD HARVEST
John Bailey	CHINA MOON
Budd Boetticher	SEMINOLE
Peter Bogdanovich	ILLEGALLY YOURS
Philip Borsos	THE MEAN SEASON
Clarence Brown	THE YEARLING
Ricou Browning	AROUND THE WORLD UNDER THE SEA, HELLO DOWN THERE
Tim Burton	EDWARD SCISSORHANDS
Edward Buzzell	NEPTUNE'S DAUGHTER
Frank Capra	A HOLE IN THE HEAD
Glen Gordon Caron	WILDER NAPALM
Joseph Cates	FAT SPY
Michael Caton-Jones	DOC HOLLYWOOD
John Cherry	ERNEST SAVES CHRISTMAS
Bob Clark	PORKY'S, PORKY'S II: THE NEXT DAY
James B. Clark	FLIPPER
Lawrence Cohen	GHOST STORY
Francis Ford Coppola	THE GODFATHER, PART II
Sean Cunningham	SPRING BREAK

Cecil B. DeMille	THE GREATEST SHOW ON EARTH
Jonathan Demme	MARRIED TO THE MOB, SOMETHING WILD
Brian De Palma	SCARFACE
Andre de Toth	SLATTERY'S HURRICANE
Richard Donner	LETHAL WEAPON 3
Gordon Douglas	FOLLOW THAT DREAM, LADY IN CEMENT, TONY ROME
Philip Dunne	BLINDFOLD
Blake Edwards	OPERATION PETTICOAT
Victor Fleming	A GUY NAMED JOE
John Ford	THEY WERE EXPENDABLE
Bob Fosse	LENNY
Lewis Foster	CROSSWINDS
John Frankenheimer	ALL FALL DOWN, BLACK SUNDAY
Howard Franklin	QUICK CHANGE
Jack Garfein	THE STRANGE ONE
Paul Michael Glaser	BAND OF THE HAND
John Glen	LICENCE TO KILL
Michael Gordon	HOW DO I LOVE THEE?
David Greenwalt	RUDE AWAKENING
Tom Gries	THE GREATEST
Edward Griffith	BAHAMA PASSAGE
Guy Hamilton	GOLDFINGER
Howard Hawks	AIR FORCE
Arthur Hiller	POPI
Kevin Hooks	PASSENGER 57
Ron Howard	COCOON, PARENTHOOD
John Hugh	YELLOWNECK
Peter Hyams	RUNNING SCARED
Jerry Jameson	AIRPORT '77
Jim Jarmusch	STRANGER THAN PARADISE
Lawrence Kasdan	BODY HEAT
Henry King	HELL HARBOR, TWELVE O'CLOCK HIGH
Randal Kleiser	FLIGHT OF THE NAVIGATOR
James Komack	PORKY'S REVENGE

Ted Kotcheff	FOLKS
John Landis	OSCAR
Carl Lerner	BLACK LIKE ME
Mervyn LeRoy	30 SECONDS OVER TOKYO
Brian Levant	PROBLEM CHILD 2
Henry Levin	WHERE THE BOYS ARE
Herschell Gordon Lewis	TWO THOUSAND MANIACS!
Jerry Lewis	THE BELLBOY
Joe Lewis	A LADY WITHOUT PASSPORT
Dick Lowry	SMOKEY AND THE BANDIT-PART 3
Anthony Mann	STRATEGIC AIR COMMAND
Daniel Mann	THE ROSE TATTOO
Michelle Manning	BLUE CITY
Alex March	PAPER LION
Leslie H. Martinson	PT-109
Andrew Marton	AROUND THE WORLD UNDER THE SEA
Elaine May	THE HEARTBREAK KID
Earl McEvoy	THE BAREFOOT MAILMAN
Thomas McGuane	92 IN THE SHADE
Chris Menges	CRISSCROSS
Howard Morris	DON'T DRINK THE WATER
Bill Murray	QUICK CHANGE
Alan Myerson	POLICE ACADEMY 5: ASSIGNMENT MIAMI BEACH
Arthur Nadel	CLAMBAKE
Hal Needham	SMOKEY AND THE BANDIT II
Paul Newman	HARRY AND SON
Mike Nichols	THE DAY OF THE DOLPHIN
Victor Nuñez	A FLASH OF GREEN, GAL YOUNG UN
David Nutter	CEASE FIRE
Arthur Penn	NIGHT MOVES
Daniel Petrie	COCOON: THE RETURN
Irving Pichel	MR. PEABODY AND THE MERMAID
Charles Pierce	THE NORSEMAN

Sydney Pollack	ABSENCE OF MALICE, HAVANA
Joe Pytka	LET IT RIDE
Harold Ramis	CADDYSHACK
Nicholas Ray	WIND ACROSS THE EVERGLADES
Carl Reiner	SUMMER RENTAL
Burt Reynolds	STICK
Michael Ritchie	SEMI-TOUGH
Martin Ritt	CROSS CREEK
Joe Roth	COUPE DE VILLE
Aaron Russo	RUDE AWAKENING
Boris Sagal	GIRL HAPPY
John Schlesinger	HONKY TONK FREEWAY, MIDNIGHT COWBOY
Martin Scorsese	CAPE FEAR
Tony Scott	DAYS OF THUNDER
Susan Seidelman	MAKING MR. RIGHT
Elliot Silverstein	THE HAPPENING
Jeannot Szwarc	JAWS 2
Richard Thorpe	ON AN ISLAND WITH YOU, TARZAN FINDS A SON!, TARZAN'S SECRET TREASURE
Gary Trousdale	BEAUTY AND THE BEAST
Raoul Walsh	DISTANT DRUMS
Charles Walters	EASY TO LOVE
Robert Webb	BENEATH THE 12 MILE REEF
Paul Wendkos	ANGEL BABY, JOHNNY TIGER
Samuel Wincer	D.A.R.Y.L.
Henry Winkler	COP AND A HALF
Kirk Wise	BEAUTY AND THE BEAST
Chuck Workman	CUBA CROSSING
Franco Zeffirelli	THE CHAMP
Howard Zieff	MY GIRL

ACTORS IN FLORIDA FILMS

Julie Adams	CREATURE FROM THE BLACK LAGOON
John Agar	REVENGE OF THE CREATURE
Eddie Albert	THE HEARTBREAK KID
Alan Alda	PAPER LION
Muhammad Ali	THE GREATEST
June Allyson	STRATEGIC AIR COMMAND
Don Ameche	COCOON, COCOON: THE RETURN, FOLKS
Alan Arkin	COUPE DE VILLE, EDWARD SCISSORHANDS, POPI
Bess Armstrong	JAWS 3-D
Elizabeth Ashley	92 IN THE SHADE
Fred Astaire	GHOST STORY
Christopher Atkins	A NIGHT IN HEAVEN
Dan Aykroyd	CADDYSHACK II, MY GIRL
Lauren Bacall	HEALTH
Jim Backus	HELLO DOWN THERE
Kathy Baker	EDWARD SCISSORHANDS
Alec Baldwin	MIAMI BLUES
Eszter Balint	STRANGER THAN PARADISE
Ellen Barkin	HARRY AND SON
Steve Bassett	SPRING BREAK
Steven Bauer	SCARFACE
Warren Beatty	ALL FALL DOWN
Robby Benson	HARRY AND SON
Candice Bergen	STICK
Milton Berle	THE BELLBOY, THE HAPPENING
Jeannie Berlin	THE HEARTBREAK KID
Bill Bixby	CLAMBAKE
Robert Blake	PT-109
Joan Blondell	ANGEL BABY

Lisa Blount	CEASE FIRE
Ann Blyth	MR. PEABODY AND THE MERMAID
Ward Bond	THEY WERE EXPENDABLE
Ernest Borgnine	THE GREATEST
Beau Bridges	HONKY TONK FREEWAY
Lloyd Bridges	AROUND THE WORLD UNDER THE SEA
Wilford Brimley	ABSENCE OF MALICE, COCOON, COCOON: THE RETURN
John Bromfield	REVENGE OF THE CREATURE
Blair Brown	A FLASH OF GREEN
Ricou Browning	CREATURE FROM THE BLACK LAGOON, REVENGE OF THE CREATURE
Carol Burnett	HEALTH
Colleen Camp	ILLEGALLY YOURS
John Candy	SUMMER RENTAL
Claudia Cardinale	BLINDFOLD
Richard Carlson	CREATURE FROM THE BLACK LAGOON
Harry Carey	AIR FORCE
Michael Carmine	BAND OF THE HAND
Leo G. Carroll	BAHAMA PASSAGE
Madeleine Carroll	BAHAMA PASSAGE
Veronica Cartwright	FLIGHT OF THE NAVIGATOR
Kim Cattral	PORKY'S
Dick Cavett	HEALTH
Ben Chapman	CREATURE FROM THE BLACK LAGOON
Cyd Charisse	ON AN ISLAND WITH YOU
Chevy Chase	CADDYSHACK
Anna Chlumsky	MY GIRL
Susan Clark	NIGHT MOVES, PORKY'S
Jill Clayburgh	SEMI-TOUGH
Chuck Connors	FLIPPER

Sean Connery	GOLDFINGER
Richard Conte	LADY IN CEMENT
Bert Convy	SEMI-TOUGH
Jackie Coogan	GIRL HAPPY
Gary Cooper	DISTANT DRUMS
Jerome Courtland	THE BAREFOOT MAILMAN
Peter Coyote	CROSS CREEK
Joey Cramer	FLIGHT OF THE NAVIGATOR
Richard Crenna	BODY HEAT,
	SUMMER RENTAL
Hume Cronyn	COCOON,
	COCOON: THE RETURN,
	HONKY TONK FREEWAY
Tom Cruise	DAYS OF THUNDER
Billy Crystal	RUNNING SCARED
Xavier Cugat	NEPTUNE'S DAUGHTER
Macaulay Culkin	MY GIRL
Robert Cummings	THE BAREFOOT MAILMAN
Jamie Lee Curtis	MY GIRL
Tony Curtis	OPERATION PETTICOAT
Timothy Dalton	BRENDA STARR,
	LICENCE TO KILL
Charles Dance	CHINA MOON
Beverly D'Angelo	HONKY TONK FREEWAY
Rodney Dangerfield	CADDYSHACK
Jeff Daniels	SOMETHING WILD
Ted Danson	BODY HEAT
Linda Darnell	SLATTERY'S HURRICANE
Geena Davis	QUICK CHANGE
Patrick Dempsey	COUPE DE VILLE
Robert De Niro	CAPE FEAR
Brian Dennehey	COCOON,
	COCOON: THE RETURN
Johnny Depp	EDWARD SCISSORHANDS
William Devane	HONKY TONK FREEWAY
Brandon De Wilde	ALL FALL DOWN
Melinda Dillon	ABSENCE OF MALICE
Phyllis Diller	FAT SPY
Brian Donlevy	FAT SPY
Vincent D'Onofrio	FIRES WITHIN

Melvin Douglas	GHOST STORY
Richard Dreyfuss	HELLO DOWN THERE, LET IT RIDE
Faye Dunaway	THE CHAMP, THE HAPPENING
Irene Dunne	A GUY NAMED JOE
Jimmy Durante	ON AN ISLAND WITH YOU
Charles Durning	STICK
Robert Duvall	DAYS OF THUNDER, THE GREATEST
Clint Eastwood	REVENGE OF THE CREATURE
Shirley Eaton	AROUND THE WORLD UNDER THE SEA, GOLDFINGER
Richard Edson	STRANGER THAN PARADISE
Vera-Ellen	THE BIG LEAGUER
Chad Everett	JOHNNY TIGER
Shelley Fabares	CLAMBAKE, GIRL HAPPY
Douglas Fairbanks, Jr.	GHOST STORY
Dolores Faith	WILD HARVEST
Mel Ferrer	THE NORSEMAN
Sally Field	ABSENCE OF MALICE, SMOKEY AND THE BANDIT II
Rhonda Fleming	CROSSWINDS
Bridgette Fonda	DOC HOLLYWOOD
Peter Fonda	92 IN THE SHADE
Michael J. Fox	DOC HOLLYWOOD
Connie Francis	WHERE THE BOYS ARE
Dean Fredericks	WILD HARVEST
Andy Garcia	THE MEAN SEASON
John Garfield	AIR FORCE
James Garner	HEALTH
Teri Garr	HONKY TONK FREEWAY, LET IT RIDE
Lorraine Gary	JAWS 2
Ben Gazzara	THE STRANGE ONE
Mel Gibson	LETHAL WEAPON 3

Jack Gilford	COCOON, COCOON: THE RETURN
Annabeth Gish	COUPE DE VILLE
Jackie Gleason	DON'T DRINK THE WATER, HOW DO I LOVE THEE?, SMOKEY AND THE BANDIT II, SMOKEY AND THE BANDIT-PART 3
Danny Glover	LETHAL WEAPON 3
Louis Gossett, Jr.	JAWS 3-D
Cary Grant	OPERATION PETTICOAT
Peter Graves	BENEATH THE 12 MILE REEF
James Gregory	PT-109
Melanie Griffith	NIGHT MOVES, SOMETHING WILD
Charles Grodin	THE HEARTBREAK KID
Arye Gross	COUPE DE VILLE
Steve Guttenberg	COCOON, COCOON: THE RETURN
Gene Hackman	NIGHT MOVES
Barbara Hale	SEMINOLE
Anthony Michael Hall	EDWARD SCISSORHANDS
Luke Halpin	FLIPPER
George Hamilton	ANGEL BABY, WHERE THE BOYS ARE
Murray Hamilton	JAWS 2
Woody Harrelson	DOC HOLLYWOOD
Ed Harris	CHINA MOON, A FLASH OF GREEN
Dolores Hart	WHERE THE BOYS ARE
Lisa Hartman	WHERE THE BOYS ARE '84
Goldie Hawn	CRISSCROSS
Sterling Hayden	BAHAMA PASSAGE
Mariel Hemingway	THE MEAN SEASON
Jean Hersholt	HELL HARBOR
Howard Hesseman	HONKY TONK FREEWAY
Charlton Heston	THE GREATEST SHOW ON EARTH
Gregory Hines	RUNNING SCARED

John Hodiak	A LADY WITHOUT PASSPORT
Dustin Hoffman	LENNY, MIDNIGHT COWBOY
John Houseman	GHOST STORY
Arliss Howard	CRISSCROSS
Rock Hudson	BLINDFOLD, SEMINOLE
Tom Hulce	PARENTHOOD
Mary Beth Hurt	D.A.R.Y.L.
William Hurt	BODY HEAT
Betty Hutton	THE GREATEST SHOW ON EARTH
Jim Hutton	WHERE THE BOYS ARE
Lauren Hutton	PAPER LION
Burl Ives	WIND ACROSS THE EVERGLADES
Glenda Jackson	HEALTH
Dean Jagger	TWELVE O'CLOCK HIGH
Claude Jarman, Jr.	THE YEARLING
Salome Jens	ANGEL BABY
David Johansen	LET IT RIDE
Don Johnson	CEASE FIRE
Van Johnson	EASY TO LOVE, A GUY NAMED JOE, 30 SECONDS OVER TOKYO
James Earl Jones	THE GREATEST
Janet Jones	POLICE ACADEMY 5: ASSIGNMENT MIAMI BEACH
Richard Jordan	A FLASH OF GREEN, THE MEAN SEASON
Alex Karras	PAPER LION, PORKY'S
Lainie Kazan	LADY IN CEMENT
Marthe Keller	BLACK SUNDAY
Emmett Kelly	THE GREATEST SHOW ON EARTH, WIND ACROSS THE EVERGLADES

Arthur Kennedy	AIR FORCE
Margo Kidder	92 IN THE SHADE
Nicole Kidman	DAYS OF THUNDER
David Knell	SPRING BREAK
Kris Kristofferson	SEMI-TOUGH
Veronica Lake	SLATTERY'S HURRICANE
Hedy Lamarr	A LADY WITHOUT PASSPORT
Dorothy Lamour	THE GREATEST SHOW ON EARTH
Burt Lancaster	THE ROSE TATTOO
Paul Land	SPRING BREAK
Perry Lang	SPRING BREAK
Stephen Lang	BAND OF THE HAND
Jessica Lange	CAPE FEAR
Peter Lawford	ON AN ISLAND WITH YOU
Gypsy Rose Lee	WIND ACROSS THE EVERGLADES
Janet Leigh	HELLO DOWN THERE
Jennifer Jason Leigh	MIAMI BLUES
Jack E. Leonard	FAT SPY
Jerry Lewis	THE BELLBOY
Juliette Lewis	CAPE FEAR
Ray Liotta	SOMETHING WILD
Robert Loggia	SCARFACE
Linda Lovelace	DEEP THROAT
Rob Lowe	ILLEGALLY YOURS
John Lurie	STRANGER THAN PARADISE
Robert Lyons	CEASE FIRE
Simon MacCorkindale	JAWS 3-D
Anna Magnani	THE ROSE TATTOO
Ann Magnuson	MAKING MR. RIGHT
George Maharis	THE HAPPENING
Lee Majors	THE NORSEMAN
John Malkovich	MAKING MR. RIGHT
Cheech Marin	RUDE AWAKENING
Steve Martin	PARENTHOOD
Tony Martin	EASY TO LOVE
Jayne Mansfield	FAT SPY
Connie Mason	TWO THOUSAND MANIACS!

Jackie Mason	CADDYSHACK II
Mary Elizabeth Mastrantonio	SCARFACE
Mercedes McCambridge	ANGEL BABY
Lin McCarthy	YELLOWNECK
Matt McCoy	POLICE ACADEMY 5: ASSIGNMENT MIAMI BEACH
Roddy McDowall	HELLO DOWN THERE
Michael McKean	D.A.R.Y.L.
Dina Merrill	OPERATION PETTICOAT
Gary Merrill	AROUND THE WORLD UNDER THE SEA, CLAMBAKE, TWELVE O'CLOCK HIGH
Laurie Metcalf	MAKING MR. RIGHT
Yvette Mimieux	WHERE THE BOYS ARE
Robert Mitchum	30 SECONDS OVER TOKYO
Ricardo Montalban	NEPTUNE'S DAUGHTER, ON AN ISLAND WITH YOU
Robert Montgomery	THEY WERE EXPENDABLE
Terry Moore	THE BAREFOOT MAILMAN, BENEATH THE 12 MILE REEF
Rick Moranis	PARENTHOOD
Rita Moreno	POPI
Gary Morton	LENNY
Roger E. Mosely	THE GREATEST, SEMI-TOUGH
Bill Murray	CADDYSHACK, QUICK CHANGE
Judd Nelson	BLUE CITY
Lori Nelson	REVENGE OF THE CREATURE
Paul Newman	ABSENCE OF MALICE, HARRY AND SON
Nick Nolte	CAPE FEAR
Warren Oates	92 IN THE SHADE
Joan O'Brien	OPERATION PETTICOAT
Arthur O'Connell	FOLLOW THAT DREAM

Maureen O'Hara	HOW DO I LOVE THEE?
Michael O'Keefe	CADDYSHACK
Barrett Oliver	COCOON,
	D.A.R.Y.L.
Maureen O'Sullivan	TARZAN FINDS A SON!,
	TARZAN'S SECRET TREASURE
Al Pacino	THE GODFATHER, PART II,
	SCARFACE
Geraldine Page	HONKY TONK FREEWAY
Sarah Jessica Parker	FLIGHT OF THE NAVIGATOR
Estelle Parsons	DOC HOLLYWOOD
John Payne	CROSSWINDS
David Peck	GAL YOUNG UN
Gregory Peck	TWELVE O'CLOCK HIGH,
	THE YEARLING
George Peppard	THE STRANGE ONE
Valerie Perrine	LENNY
Martha Plimpton	PARENTHOOD
Christopher	
Plummer	WIND ACROSS THE
	EVERGLADES
William Powell	MR. PEABODY AND THE
	MERMAID
Michelle Pfeiffer	MARRIED TO THE MOB,
	SCARFACE
Paula Prentiss	WHERE THE BOYS ARE
Elvis Presley	CLAMBAKE,
	FOLLOW THAT DREAM,
	GIRL HAPPY
Robert Preston	SEMI-TOUGH
Dana Preu	GAL YOUNG UN
Vincent Price	EDWARD SCISSORHANDS
Dennis Quaid	JAWS 3-D
Randy Quaid	DAYS OF THUNDER,
	QUICK CHANGE
Anthony Quinn	THE HAPPENING,
	SEMINOLE
Tony Randall	HELLO DOWN THERE
Robert Redford	HAVANA
Donna Reed	THEY WERE EXPENDABLE

Jerry Reed	SMOKEY AND THE BANDIT II
Keanu Reeves	PARENTHOOD
Alejandro Rey	BLINDFOLD
Burt Reynolds	ANGEL BABY,
	COP AND A HALF,
	SEMI-TOUGH,
	SMOKEY AND THE BANDIT II,
	STICK
John Ritter	PROBLEM CHILD 2
Thelma Ritter	A HOLE IN THE HEAD
John Ridgely	AIR FORCE
Jason Robards	PARENTHOOD,
	QUICK CHANGE
Eric Roberts	RUDE AWAKENING
Cliff Robertson	PT-109
Dar Robinson	STICK
Edward G. Robinson	THE BIG LEAGUER,
	A HOLE IN THE HEAD
Mickey Rourke	BODY HEAT
Gena Rowlands	TONY ROME
Kurt Russell	THE MEAN SEASON
Winona Ryder	EDWARD SCISSORHANDS
Jill St. John	TONY ROME
Greta Scacchi	FIRES WITHIN
Roy Scheider	JAWS 2
Ricky Schroder	THE CHAMP
George C. Scott	THE DAY OF THE DOLPHIN
George Segal	STICK
Tom Selleck	FOLKS
Robert Shaw	BLACK SUNDAY
Ally Sheedy	BLUE CITY
Brooke Shields	BRENDA STARR
Cybill Shepherd	THE HEARTBREAK KID
Frank Sinatra	A HOLE IN THE HEAD,
	LADY IN CEMENT,
	TONY ROME
Red Skelton	NEPTUNE'S DAUGHTER
Bubba Smith	POLICE ACADEMY 5:
	ASSIGNMENT
	MIAMI BEACH

Jimmy Smits	FIRES WITHIN
Wesley Snipes	PASSENGER 57
Sylvester Stallone	OSCAR
Harry Dean Stanton	92 IN THE SHADE
Maureen Stapleton	COCOON, COCOON: THE RETURN
Mary Steenburgen	CROSS CREEK, PARENTHOOD
Daniel Stern	COUPE DE VILLE
David Ogden Stiers	DOC HOLLYWOOD
James Stewart	AIR FORCE, THE GREATEST SHOW ON EARTH, STRATEGIC AIR COMMAND
Dean Stockwell	MARRIED TO THE MOB
Madeleine Stowe	CHINA MOON
Lee Strasberg	THE GODFATHER, PART II
Jessica Tandy	COCOON, COCOON: THE RETURN, HONKY TONK FREEWAY
Robert Taylor	JOHNNY TIGER
Leah Thompson	JAWS 3-D
Rip Torn	CROSS CREEK, SUMMER RENTAL
Spencer Tracy	A GUY NAMED JOE, 30 SECONDS OVER TOKYO
Forrest Tucker	CROSSWINDS
Kathleen Turner	BODY HEAT
Jim Varney	ERNEST SAVES CHRISTMAS
Robert Vaughn	CUBA CROSSING
Lupe Velez	HELL HARBOR
Jon Voight	THE CHAMP, MIDNIGHT COWBOY
Robert Wagner	BENEATH THE 12 MILE REEF
Robert Walker	30 SECONDS OVER TOKYO
Robert Walker, Jr.	THE HAPPENING
Fred Ward	MIAMI BLUES
Jack Warden	BLINDFOLD, THE CHAMP
Julie Warner	DOC HOLLYWOOD

Jennifer Warren	NIGHT MOVES
Leslie Ann Warren	A NIGHT IN HEAVEN
John Wayne	THEY WERE EXPENDABLE
Johnny Weissmuller	TARZAN FINDS A SON!, TARZAN'S SECRET TREASURE
Raquel Welch	LADY IN CEMENT
Richard Widmark	SLATTERY'S HURRICANE
Stuart Whitman	CUBA CROSSING
James Whitmore	BLACK LIKE ME
Dianne Wiest	EDWARD SCISSORHANDS, PARENTHOOD
Cornel Wilde	THE NORSEMAN
Esther Williams	EASY TO LOVE, NEPTUNE'S DAUGHTER, ON AN ISLAND WITH YOU
Paul Winfield	BLUE CITY, THE GREATEST
Michael Winslow	POLICE ACADEMY 5: ASSIGNMENT MIAMI BEACH
Shelley Winters	HOW DO I LOVE THEE?
Alfre Woodard	CROSS CREEK, HEALTH
Joanne Woodward	HARRY AND SON
Thomas Wood	TWO THOUSAND MANIACS!
James Woods	NIGHT MOVES
Jane Wyman	THE YEARLING
Keenan Wynn	AROUND THE WORLD UNDER THE SEA, NEPTUNE'S DAUGHTER
Gig Young	AIR FORCE

ACADEMY AWARDS

It is a rarely known axiom of filmmaking that a sure-fire way to secure an Academy Award for Best Picture is to combine Florida and mass transit. For example, *It Happened One Night*, though not filmed in the Sunshine State, begins on a bus in Florida, and it was the first film to sweep all the major Oscars. *The Greatest Show on Earth*, set and shot in Florida, ends with a train wreck, and was the surprise Best Picture winner for 1952. *Midnight Cowboy* ends on a bus in Miami, and the film went on to become the only X-rated film to win a Best Picture Oscar.

If not properly observed, the Florida Mass Transit Oscar Rule can rob a deserving film of its award. Although many consider *Citizen Kane* the greatest film of all time, it did not win a Best Picture Oscar. Perhaps this is because in the opening scene, which is set in Florida, Kane whispers "Rosebud," which is the name of his sled. Everyone knows that a sled makes lousy mass transportation, especially in Florida.

The following is a list of Florida films and performances that have been honored by the Academy as award nominees and winners. Only films that were shot in Florida, and performances that were filmed there, are included.

BEST PICTURE

Winners
THE GODFATHER, PART II
THE GREATEST SHOW ON EARTH
MIDNIGHT COWBOY

Nominees
BEAUTY AND THE BEAST
LENNY
TWELVE O'CLOCK HIGH
THE YEARLING

BEST ACTOR

Nominees

Robert De Niro	CAPE FEAR
Dustin Hoffman	LENNY
Dustin Hoffman	MIDNIGHT COWBOY
Paul Newman	ABSENCE OF MALICE
Al Pacino	THE GODFATHER, PART II
Gregory Peck	TWELVE O'CLOCK HIGH
Gregory Peck	THE YEARLING
Jon Voight	MIDNIGHT COWBOY

BEST ACTRESS

Winner

Anna Magnani	THE ROSE TATTOO

Nominees

Valerie Perrine	LENNY
Jane Wyman	THE YEARLING

BEST SUPPORTING ACTOR

Winners

Don Ameche	COCOON
Dean Jagger	TWELVE O'CLOCK HIGH

Nominees

Eddie Albert	THE HEARTBREAK KID
Lee Strasberg	THE GODFATHER, PART II
Rip Torn	CROSS CREEK

BEST SUPPORTING ACTRESS

Nominees

Jeannie Berlin	THE HEARTBREAK KID
Melinda Dillon	ABSENCE OF MALICE
Juliette Lewis	CAPE FEAR
Dianne Wiest	PARENTHOOD
Alfre Woodard	CROSS CREEK

REFERENCES

Barth, Jack. *Roadside Hollywood*. Contemporary Books. (Chicago: 1991)

Bergan, Ronald. *The United Artists Story*. Crown Publishers. (New York: 1986)

Eagan, Daniel, ed. *HBO's Guide to Movies on Videocassette and Cable TV*. Harper Perennial. (New York: 1991)

Eames, John Douglas. *The MGM Story*. Crown Publishers. (New York: 1986)

Eames, John Douglas. *The Paramount Story*. Crown Publishers. (New York: 1985)

Eastman, John. *Retakes: Behind the Scenes of 500 Classic Movies*. Ballantine Books. (New York: 1989)

Ebert, Roger. *Roger Ebert's Movie Home Companion, 1990 Edition*. Andrews and McMeel. (Kansas City: 1989)

Freedland, Michael. *Gregory Peck*. William Morrow and Company. (New York: 1980)

Garland, Brock. *War Movies*. Facts on File Publications. (New York: 1987)

Glut, Donald. *Classic Movie Monsters*. The Scarecrow Press. (Metuchen, N.J.: 1978)

Hay, Peter. *MGM When The Lion Roars*. Turner Publishing. (Atlanta: 1991)

Halliwell, Leslie. *Halliwell's Film Guide, Sixth Edition*. Charles Scribner's Sons. (New York: 1987)

Higham, Charles. *Cecil B. DeMille*. Scribner and Sons. (New York: 1973)

Hirschhorn, Clive. *The Universal Story*. Crown Publishers. (New York: 1983)

Katz, Ephraim. *The Film Encyclopedia*. Perigee Books. (New York: 1979)

Maltin, Leonard, ed. *Leonard Maltin's TV Movies and Video Guide 1992 Edition*. Signet Books. (New York: 1992)

Nash, Jay Robert and Ross, Stanley Ralph. *The Motion Picture Guide*. Cinebooks, Inc. (Chicago: 1986)

Nelson, Nancy. *Evenings with Cary Grant*. William Morrow and Company. (New York: 1991)

Nelson, Richard Allen. *Lights, Camera, Florida!*. Florida Endowment for the Humanities. (Tampa: 1987)

Novak, Ralph and Travers, Peter, ed. *People Magazine Guide to Movies on Video*. Collier Books. (New York: 1987)

Oumano, Elena. *Paul Newman*. St. Martin's Press. (New York: 1989)

Sackett, Susan. *Box Office Hits*. Billboard Books. (New York: 1990)

Thomas, Tony. *The Films of 20th Century-Fox*. Citadel Press. (Secaucus, N.J.: 1985)

Tolf, Robert and Russell Buchan. *Florida Weekends*. Potter. (New York: 1990)

Wayne, Jane Ellen. *Cooper's Women*. Prentice Hall. (New York: 1988)